Getting your S/NVQ

A guide for candidates in the information and library sector

Second edition

JUSTIN ARUNDALE

LIBRARY ASSOCIATION PUBLISHING
LONDON

PUBLISHED IN ASSOCIATION WITH
THE INFORMATION AND LIBRARY
SERVICES LEAD BODY

Published by
Library Association Publishing
7 Ridgmount Street
London WC1E 7AE

Library Association Publishing is wholly owned by The Library Association.

First published 1996
This second edition 1999

British Library Cataloguing in Publication Data
A catalogue record is available from the British Library.

ISBN 1-85604-289-8

Library Association Publishing offer their grateful thanks for the support of the Department for Education and Employment (DfEE) for this publication.

Typeset in 12/14pt Elegant Garamond and Arial by Library Association Publishing.
Printed and made in Great Britain by Bell & Bain Ltd, Glasgow.

To May, who taught me

Contents

Acknowledgments

This book would have been impossible to write, and subsequently to revise, without the help and support of many people. I should like to thank in particular Heather Saddleton, who kindly shared with me her experience of assessing and managing NVQs, and Paul Scarsbrook and Angela Frampton, who kept me informed about changes in procedures, as well as about candidate and assessor feedback. David Whitaker and Hazel Dakers, respectively the first Chairman and first Assistant Project Manager of the Lead Body, have offered much patient and good-humoured encouragement. I am also indebted to members of staff of all of the awarding bodies for their advice and assistance in untangling some of the bureaucratic and terminological knots.

I am grateful to OCR for permission to make use of a number of RSA documents including their invaluable *Notes for Guidance – National Vocational Qualifications*. The material in the Figures in Chapter 3 and Appendix 1 is copyright of the Information and Library Services Lead Body. The table on page 109 is copyright of QCA. Both are reproduced by kind permission.

I must also thank my friends and colleagues at the School of Information Management of the University of Brighton for putting up with my prolonged absences and my obsession with S/NVQs.

Introduction

Since the publication of the first edition of this book, National and Scottish Vocational Qualifications (NVQs and SVQs) have become an established part of the information and library scene. In the summer of 1995, when the first set of standards and the first NVQs and SVQs that derive from them were approved, they were still unfamiliar and, indeed, controversial. Since then, an increasing number of employers have been recognizing and encouraging the qualifications, and an increasing number of candidates have been using NVQs and SVQs as a way of gaining recognition of their working skills. However, if the qualifications are to remain relevant, it is important that they are kept up to date – and it is an essential requirement of the S/NVQ system that the standards underpinning the qualifications are revised regularly. Consequently, in early 1999, an updated set of standards were published. At the same time, the original awarding bodies for NVQs and SVQs in information and library services changed – the RSA changed its name to OCR, and was joined by Edexcel, and SCOTVEC was succeeded by SQA. As a result, the qualifications available to candidates who register after the beginning of 1999 are somewhat different in form from those that we have become used to, and they are administered by different organizations.

This revised edition reflects those changes. First, I have rewritten the description of the standards (particularly in Chapters 3 and 4) to take account of the revisions in content and presentation of the revised standards documentation.

Second, I have revised the text throughout to reflect the changes, both in terms of the standards and of the administration of the qualifications, that have taken place since 1995. In particular, I have taken account of the small differences in procedure and terminology that exist between the three different awarding bodies.

A word needs to be said for the benefit of any readers who registered for an NVQ or SVQ – or one of the constituent Units – under the old, unrevised, standards. Provided that you complete your qualification (or Unit) within two years (for Level 2) or three years (for Levels 3 and 4), you will normally continue to work with the original standards that have applied since 1995. However, if you particularly want to work with the new standards, you should discuss your assessment plans with your assessor. Although you cannot simply transfer from one set of standards to other, it may be possible for you to upgrade your Units by submitting additional evidence that you meet the new standards. This second course of action obviously means that your qualification will reflect the most up-to-date version of the standards of competence.

This book has been written as a guide to what you, as a current or potential NVQ or SVQ candidate, need to know and do in order to become vocationally qualified under the revised standards. It also attempts to help you understand a bit about the theory, philosophy and methodology that lie behind vocational qualifications, and the changes that have taken place since ILS S/NVQs were introduced. If you are already working towards one of these qualifications, you may be curious to see how the standards have changed in which case Chapters 3 and 4 will be of particular interest to you.

Terminology

One word about terminology. The system for vocational qualifications operates throughout the United Kingdom in exactly the same way – using the same standards and basic procedures everywhere. However, in Scotland the administrative system and the terminology are different. There, the whole structure is run by a body called the Scottish Qualifications Agency (SQA), which awards Scottish Vocational Qualifications (SVQs) – while in England, Wales and Northern Ireland, National Vocational Qualifications (NVQs) are awarded in a system overseen by an organization known as the Qualifications and Curriculum Authority (QCA). Nevertheless, NVQs and SVQs are, in effect, interchangeable, and awards made in one country of the UK are recognized everywhere else. You will often find these qualifications referred to as S/NVQs (for Scottish and/or National Vocational Qualifications), and I have followed this convention. So every reference to S/NVQs includes both NVQs and SVQs unless I have specifically made a distinction between them.

Structure of this book

In **Chapter 1** you will find an overview of S/NVQs – what they are, and how they relate to the existing systems of qualifications. You will also look closely at one of the most important S/NVQ jargon words – 'competence' – and see how the close relationship between S/NVQs and the world of employment is defined.

Chapter 2 introduces you to the assessment system – the S/NVQ equivalent of examinations, if you wish. The various institutions and individuals you will encounter as you pass through the S/NVQ system are described and their functions explained.

In **Chapter 3** you will find an account of the revised standards upon which S/NVQs are based. You will learn how to 'read' a standard, which is a very important part of discovering what it is you will be expected to do in order to get your S/NVQ.

Chapter 4 is all about evidence – what evidence you need to collect in order to demonstrate that you have achieved the necessary standards to be awarded an S/NVQ.

Chapter 5 looks at how to create, organize and index a portfolio of evidence.

By the time you have worked your way through the book you should have gained a good understanding of how S/NVQs work. **Chapter 6** is therefore about what to do next and how to get started.

After the main chapters of the book you will find two reference sections. **Section A** gives the addresses and contact details of the main organizations involved in ILS S/NVQs. **Section B** is a glossary – a 'jargon-buster' – to help you keep track of all the acronyms and words with special meanings in S/NVQ-speak.

There are two appendices. The first, **Appendix 1**, reproduces in full the text of the assessment guidance notes which form part of the national standards. These notes are aimed at assessors, but are very useful for candidates as well. **Appendix 2** is for those who would like to look a little further into the S/NVQ process. It is about the development and revision of S/NVQ standards, and how the principles of what is known as 'functional analysis' have been applied to our work sector.

1 What are S/NVQs?

In this chapter we look at some of the
characteristics of S/NVQs that make them
different from traditional qualifications, and
begin to see why they are important in
information and library services.

Qualifications are about measurement

We all need ways of measuring what we, and other people
around us, can do. When you were at school or college, you
wanted to measure what you had learned, to demonstrate your
ability to employers, family and friends. Your teachers and
trainers needed to measure the success of their efforts to transfer skills and knowledge.

Now, as an employee, you want to measure your skills, to
see how good you are at your present work – and, sooner or
later, to demonstrate that you have the skills and experience
needed for a new and more demanding job. Your present and
future employers need to measure what job applicants can do
before they are recruited – and to keep track of how staff are
progressing and what skills they are learning. Even governments need to measure what skills are present in the country
– and which ones are absent – to help with economic planning. Qualifications are one of the ways of measuring for all
these purposes – and the good ones will measure fairly and
honestly, without discrimination or bias.

However, any qualification is of limited use unless everyone understands exactly what it is that has been measured. The most widely recognized qualifications are the ones which are most widely understood. For example, most universities recognize A-levels as a way of measuring whether applicants are suitable for their courses. This doesn't necessarily mean that A-levels are the right qualifications for the purpose – merely that they are widely understood and universally recognized. So one of the important aspects of qualifications is that they should be recognized and understood.

Qualifications set standards

But qualifications are not only about measurement. They are also about standards – setting and maintaining standards, and perhaps improving them as well. If companies or industries – or countries – use the wrong qualifications, then they can find themselves measuring the wrong skills – skills which are irrelevant or out-of-date. It has always been a criticism of the UK's qualification systems that they have tended to emphasize theoretical learning at the expense of practical skills, favouring people who can pass exams against those who can do real jobs and produce goods and services. The same criticism has also been made about qualifications in information and library work – that they favour graduates who have received theoretical training and fail to recognize the extensive practical and experience-based skills of many non-graduate staff.

•••

Qualifications should:
• measure skills and achievements
• be widely recognized
• set standards.

•••

During the past 15 years, successive governments have been addressing the national 'qualifications problem' by working with employers, training institutions and professional bodies to bring some kind of order to the diverse systems that have arisen in the UK. These efforts are intended to lead towards a national framework in which different qualifications can be related to each other in a way which is clear and easy to understand. But they are also intended to create a structure which integrates together qualifications such as those gained at school and college with ones which are profession- or craft-related, so that there is a clear route which leads people forward from school into the complex and demanding world of employment.

National and Scottish Vocational Qualifications

In response to this, a large committee of experienced librarians, information scientists and information managers has sought to address the same 'qualifications problem' in our own sector. Its efforts have led to the development and, more recently, the revision of a set of national standards for those working in information and library services in the UK, which can act as a guide to quality and competence for both employers and employees. These standards have also become the basis for the first National and Scottish Vocational Qualifications in our area of employment.

National and Scottish Vocational Qualifications are a very important component of the UK's qualifications system, because they deal with measuring skills that are directly relevant to the real day-to-day world of work. But they are also important because of the way in which they encourage people to move forward. First, they assist people to move from school and college into a working environment. Then they help people develop their working careers by providing a clear route forward, allowing developing skills and maturity to be acknowledged and recognized. This process is referred to as **progression** – S/NVQs, in this sense, are highly progressive qualifications.

S/NVQs are designed to be:
- **fair and universal across the country**
- **related to the real world of employment**
- **accessible to everyone**
- **progressive.**

So S/NVQs have come into existence to meet the need for a system which measures work-related skills fairly and consistently, which is easy to understand because it is the same everywhere, which is related to the real needs of employers and employees, which is progressive – and which is accessible to everyone. S/NVQs cover a huge range of skill areas – from management to accountancy and from journalism to child care – within a single system and with a common philosophy – and an S/NVQ in book-keeping, for example, will have been gained in much the same way as one in press photography or working with pre-school children. Let us look at some of these characteristics in a little more detail.

S/NVQs are employment based

S/NVQs do not measure theoretical knowledge. They are concerned with the skills used in the workplace. They are concerned with the ability to do a job satisfactorily and to an agreed standard. Within the S/NVQ system the term used to refer to these skills is 'competence'. S/NVQs measure competence – and job-competence or competence in the workplace specifically. Competence, after all, is what matters most in employment. Employees need to be competent if they are to keep and develop their present jobs and progress to more ambitious work in the future. Employers need competent employees if their objectives are to be met and jobs and prosperity secured for all members of their organizations. And, indeed, the country needs competent citizens if our national competitiveness is to be maintained.

The fact that S/NVQs are employment-based means that they are ideally suited for people whose skills and knowledge have been acquired through work experience. Most people learn at least some of their work-related skills by doing a job, as well as through being trained or taught. These important skills may be easy to recognize, but they are often difficult to measure. S/NVQs are designed specifically to measure skills as they are exercised in a working environment – irrespective of how the skills have been acquired.

This link between S/NVQs and work-related competence has led many people to believe that they are qualifications designed only for craft or industrial environments. Many people associate S/NVQs exclusively with 'blue-collar' trades such as hairdressing, building construction or steel-making. It is true that S/NVQs started in these areas, but it was always the intention that they should spread into the traditionally 'white-collar' trades and professions – and this is exactly what has happened. Earlier in this chapter I referred at random to S/NVQs in child care, journalism and management. I could equally have chosen pensions administration, business counselling or insurance – all employment sectors where the new qualifications have been introduced and are being used.

••

S/NVQs measure competence at work. They are concerned with the skills used in the workplace, and with the ability to do a job competently and to an agreed standard.

••

S/NVQs assist career progression

Most people's careers develop as they gain experience and move into more complex jobs with wider responsibilities. The S/NVQ system assists this process, because it enables people to gain recognition for their widening skills as their experience increases. So an S/NVQ gained in one job, which measures and recognizes the competence built up through that period of work experience, can also provide the impetus for moving on towards a more complex, probably more senior, job. Thus S/NVQs both recognize and give credit for developing skills, and also provide a way of turning developing skills into a developing career.

The easiest way of understanding how S/NVQs help career progression is to look at how they are organized. Within the S/NVQ system there are five levels which recognize attainments from the application of basic skills to a high degree of professional understanding. They are numbered from 1 to 5 (although at present ILS S/NVQs exist only at Levels 2, 3 and 4). At each level qualifications are made up of subdivisions known as Units, each of which requires you to show that you are competent in a particular area of work. As your career progresses and you gain more experience and learn more skills, you can collect new Units – and if you gain all of the Units comprising a particular S/NVQ, then you have gained the S/NVQ. You will find out more about Units in Chapter 3.

The S/NVQ structure therefore assists your career progression by allowing you to gain recognition as you acquire skills through normal work experience. But it also makes it easier to plan for your future, by helping you identify areas where your skills are weak or need developing, and by allowing you to work towards gaining Unit recognition in those areas. It may be that in order to gain a Unit you have selected, you will need extra training or even additional experience of working in a

new area of your organization. But once you have demonstrated competence, and gained the Unit, your skills will have
been permanently enhanced and you will have taken another
step towards a higher level qualification and, perhaps, a more
responsible and senior job.

••

S/NVQs assist career progression by allowing
people to gain recognition for the skills they
already possess or acquire through work
experience, and by helping them identify areas
where they need to learn or develop new skills.

••

S/NVQs assist the transferability of skills

The S/NVQ system has been designed so that it is, as far as
possible, consistent across all areas of employment. In other
words, a Level 3 S/NVQ will have the same value and signif-
icance, irrespective of which trade, industry or profession it
refers to. Moreover, all S/NVQs are acquired in much the
same way, and their holders will have had to demonstrate
competence in doing a job. This gives both employers and
employees a way of assessing and comparing the skill levels of
people working in different areas of employment, without
having to become familiar with a whole host of different and
often incompatible qualifications and training traditions.

But S/NVQs also require candidates to demonstrate that
they are competent in relation to standards which are openly
published and the same everywhere. This means that if you
have an S/NVQ, you have demonstrated competence not only
to your employer's satisfaction, but also to the satisfaction of
an assessor working with the national standards. This
approach allows employees to gain recognition for skills
acquired in one context or job in a form which shows that they
could be applied in another, possibly very different, context.

The effect of this is to make it much easier for people to change jobs between one organization and another, or to progress from one job to another within an organization. The term used for this is 'transferability' – S/NVQ-validated skills should be transferable from place to place, and from context to context, to aid job mobility and to encourage sharing and improvement of skills across employment sectors.

Incidentally, our S/NVQ system in the UK is also designed to be compatible with similar systems elsewhere in the European Union. This means that S/NVQ-validated skills can be transferred abroad, making job mobility within Europe a great deal easier.

S/NVQs are based on open, published standards which are part of a national qualifications structure and related to other European structures. They are therefore widely recognized, making it easier for people to demonstrate their skills when they move jobs within and between sectors – and abroad.

S/NVQs in Information and Library Services (ILS)

One of the characteristics of our sector is the enormous diversity of sizes and types of libraries and information units. There are, of course, the public and academic libraries – but there are also hosts of different special and commercial libraries, with units varying in size from one to several hundred people. In all, including voluntary workers, about 110,000 people work in the sector – of whom only about 25% hold a library-related degree or other qualification.

S/NVQs have been introduced into this sector, and they are having an important impact. A great deal of information work, at all levels, is about the application of specific skills, both practical and intellectual. Some of these skills are acquired through learning, but many are gained on the job – through work-based training or experience. S/NVQs provide a means of recognizing all these skills, allowing staff at all levels to build qualifications that allow them to demonstrate to present and future employers that they are capable, competent and familiar with a wide range of work-based activities.

But while our sector is enormously diverse, there are many processes, procedures and principles which apply very widely or even universally. The ILS S/NVQ standards recognize this by defining competence in a way that is as far as possible independent of the immediate context of any particular library. This means that competence acquired in one place – and recognized by means of an S/NVQ – can be applied in another place. Information workers at all levels can demonstrate competence in a general skill area, rather than having to point to specific experience within a particular system. As a result, it is much easier for everyone – employers and employees alike – to recognize when an individual has the skills and abilities needed for a particular job.

Example

Let me illustrate this point with an example. Imagine a library assistant who has had extensive counter and back office experience in a public library, and who wants to apply for a job in a small commercial library. Instead of having to argue that public-library counter procedures are directly related to the work of a small specialist unit, this person can point to specific S/NVQ credits which recognize competence in dealing with customers, with basic enquiry and loans procedures and with the procedures for maintaining computerized data. As a result, the written job application looks more convincing and the chances of getting the new job are much improved. Moreover, our imaginary library assistant can produce some important career development reasons for wanting to make the change – that the new job will allow access to the experience which will lead to a specific new S/NVQ Unit credit. In this case we can see S/NVQs doing what they are supposed to do – recognizing skills gained in employment in a way that allows them to be transferred to another kind of job, and in a way that enhances an individual's career progression.

> In library and information services, S/NVQs make it easier to learn skills in one kind of library and apply them in another. Job mobility and career progression are both made simpler.

Competence

Earlier in this chapter we saw that the S/NVQ system is about competence – that is, it attempts to measure how well you can perform a particular function or series of functions, and therefore how well you can do a particular job. The fact that it is about competence has three important implications:

- it is about *doing* a job, not describing how it should be done
- it is about doing a *real* job, in a real working environment
- it is about doing a job to a *standard* that is clearly defined and universally applied.

Doing a job

Competence is the condition of being capable of performing a task. In order to perform a task, you must possess certain skills (which may be physical or intellectual skills), and you must also possess the knowledge and judgment necessary to understand how and when to exercise them. And the best way of demonstrating that you are competent to perform a task is actually to go ahead and do it. If you complete the task satisfactorily, perhaps in a range of different situations, then you will have gone most of the way towards showing that you are competent.

By stressing the idea of competence, S/NVQs shift the emphasis in qualifications away from abstract theory and on to job performance. This is not to say that theoretical knowledge is dismissed or ignored – as we shall see, S/NVQs pay great attention to the need to understand. It simply means that these qualifications – unlike many that are more traditionally exam- or test-based – are about the practicalities of how you perform when faced with a task to do or a problem to solve.

Doing a real job

S/NVQs are closely related at every stage to the circumstances of employment. They are employment-led qualifications. That means that they measure competence in the jobs that employees actually do and employers want done. It follows that they have to measure competence by looking at how people perform in real jobs. The whole S/NVQ system is based around the idea that you demonstrate competence by showing that you are doing – or have done in the recent past – a job or task requiring the skills being measured.

This does not necessarily mean that you have to be currently employed in order to gain an S/NVQ. If you can produce evidence that you have acquired and exercised skills in the past, that may be enough. Similarly, jobs undertaken on a voluntary basis can provide you with the evidence you need. Under certain circumstances it may even be possible for you to demonstrate competence by working through simulations – where the circumstances of a real job are 'mocked up' for the purpose of testing your performance. But, although you do not have to be currently employed, you do have to be able to demonstrate that you are capable of performing tasks in the real world of work.

Doing a job to a certain standard

There is no point in a qualification that does not demand that you achieve a defined standard. In the case of S/NVQs, your performance is measured against a set of standards which define exactly what is meant by 'competence' in every area of work to which they refer. These standards are published, and everyone gaining an S/NVQ will have had to demonstrate competence to exactly the same standard.

We shall see later how the standards in information and library services operate. At this stage it is sufficient to under-stand that they are universal across the whole ILS sector – any 'information work' S/NVQ will have been measured against the same standards as any other – and comparable across all employment sectors. That means that an S/NVQ Unit demonstrates competence in a particular area of work, wher-ever that work is being carried out; and the qualification is valid whether the work is undertaken in an information unit, a library – or some entirely different area of employment.

••
Competence is about doing a real job, in a real working environment, to a standard that is clearly defined and universally applied.
••

Essential characteristics of S/NVQs

If you have read this chapter carefully, you will now under-stand some of the essential characteristics of National and Scottish Vocational Qualifications. Briefly, they are:

- *National*: they apply across the whole of the UK (although, of course, they are called SVQs in Scotland), with standards and systems that are openly published and universally applied;
- *Vocational*: they are to do with your ability to do a job, because they measure practical competence and are not based on theory;
- *Qualifications*: they recognize your practical achievements, giving you a way of demonstrating the skills you acquire as your career develops, and a way of acquiring more.

In this chapter we have looked at qualifications in general and National and Scottish Vocational Qualifications in particular. We have seen how S/NVQs are different from many of our more familiar qualifications because they are related firmly to the working environment and the world of employment. S/NVQs are about competence – and we have begun to see what competence is and how it might be measured. In the next chapter we will look at the measurement process in more detail.

2 How the S/NVQ system is organized

In this chapter we will look at how the S/NVQ system works. You will be introduced to the organizations that are involved in delivering S/NVQs in Information and Library Services, and find out about the part played by the different individuals whom you will encounter as you pass through the system.

The institutions

Behind our S/NVQs in Information and Library Services (ILS) lies a complicated bureaucracy, which is designed to ensure three very simple things:

- *comparability*: that ILS S/NVQs fit into the national qualifications framework without any anomalies or discrepancies, and can therefore be directly compared with S/NVQs in other sectors;
- *relevance*: that our S/NVQs are based on standards that are directly relevant to what is required in the workplace – in libraries and information units all round the country;
- *quality assurance*: that the standards are applied in exactly the same way for all candidates, so that an ILS S/NVQ always has the same value, no matter where it was acquired.

These three things are very important to candidates, because they guarantee the value of S/NVQs – so it is worth taking a few moments to understand how the bureaucracy works. Also, if you know which are the major institutions involved in S/NVQs and what their roles are, it will help avoid confusion later, when you come across references to them. The first part of this chapter therefore lists the most important organizations (or types of organization) concerned with S/NVQs, and briefly explains what they do.

QCA and SQA

These are the two organizations that have been set up by the Government to develop and run vocational qualifications for all of the UK. **QCA** is the Qualifications and Curriculum Authority, and covers England, Wales and Northern Ireland, while Scotland is the responsibility of **SQA**, the Scottish Qualifications Authority. The awards made by SQA are known as SVQs (Scottish Vocational Qualifications). As far as candidates and potential candidates for both SVQs and NVQs are concerned, the role of these organizations breaks down into two parts. They:

- administer the system and provide information and publicity about S/NVQs generally;
- accredit all of the qualifications, checking that standards are maintained and that different S/NVQs are consistent with each other.

One of the requirements of QCA and SQA – and therefore one of the 'rules' of the S/NVQ system – is that different S/NVQs should share Units wherever possible. This means that S/NVQs in one work sector will often 'borrow' parts of other S/NVQs which happen to be relevant or useful. For example, many jobs in libraries have some requirement for competence in dealing with customers. But there are already S/NVQs – quite separate from our own – in Customer Services. The parts of our S/NVQs that relate to looking after customers have therefore been 'borrowed' from the Customer Services S/NVQs. QCA and SQA set the rules for procedures like this, that involve more than one area of work.

....

QCA and SQA administer the system of NVQs and SVQs and accredit all of the qualifications delivered.

....

The lead body

In developing S/NVQ standards, QCA relies on organizations known as standard-setting bodies, or **lead bodies.** There is one lead body for each employment sector for which S/NVQs exist or are being developed. They are usually large committees made up of experienced managers and workers from all parts of the sector, which are responsible for developing and regularly revising the written standards upon which the sector's S/NVQs are based. In the case of information and library services, the lead body brought together senior librarians, information scientists and information managers, along with specialists in areas such as indexing, archive management and tourist information.

The most important thing produced by our lead body – the ILS Lead Body – has been the set of national standards of competence in information and library services, originally published in 1995 and subsequently revised in 1998. These standards are not only designed to act as a yardstick for measuring the competence of S/NVQ candidates. They are also intended to be a manual of good practice. By analysing and 'benchmarking' all of the functions undertaken in libraries and information units, the lead body has tried to define what standards of performance should be expected – not just from S/NVQ candidates, but from everyone working in the sector.

....

The ILS Lead Body has developed the occupational standards in the ILS sector upon which our S/NVQs are based. It will continue to maintain the standards and keep them up to date.
....

Awarding bodies

S/NVQs are actually awarded to candidates by organizations approved by the lead body and by QCA and SQA. These organizations are known as **awarding bodies**, and they administer the entire assessment process. They are also responsible for quality control, making sure that candidates are all being fairly measured against the same standards. For ILS S/NVQs, the awarding bodies at present are Oxford Cambridge RSA Examinations (OCR) and the Edexcel Foundation for England, Wales and Northern Ireland, and SQA itself for Scotland. SQA, unlike its English counterpart QCA, is both an accrediting organization and an awarding body.

It is important to stress that the S/NVQ system applies throughout the United Kingdom. NVQs in England and their Scottish equivalents, SVQs, are in effect interchangeable. Both sets of qualifications are measured against the same standards, which do not vary between the different countries of the UK, and the methods of assessment are virtually identical. So an SVQ gained in Scotland will have exactly the same validity and status as an NVQ gained in England. It is even possible to gain an English NVQ where some of the Units have been awarded in Scotland under the SVQ system – and, of course, vice versa.

Awarding bodies also have the very important function of issuing Certificates to successful candidates – either for a full S/NVQ or for single Units.

....

Our awarding bodies, OCR, Edexcel and SQA, are responsible for overseeing the detailed NVQ and SVQ procedures, ensuring that quality is maintained and actually awarding the qualifications to successful candidates.

....

Assessment centres

Here we reach the last link in the chain between the various bodies that develop, accredit and award S/NVQs and the candidates. **Assessment centres,** as their name suggests, are the organizations that undertake the actual measurement of individual candidates' competence against the standards and within the procedures laid down for them. They are approved by an awarding body. Before they can be approved as assessment centres, organizations have to go through a process of registration, in which they have to demonstrate that they have the right procedures in place and staff with the appropriate training and experience to assess candidates fairly. In other words, assessment centres themselves have to be assessed.

In spite of the word 'centre', an assessment centre is not necessarily a single physical location – indeed, it may not even be a single organization. Many ILS assessment centres are companies or local authorities, assessing candidates in all sorts of different places. Some are colleges or training centres, and others are consortia – where a number of organizations have banded together to offer assessment facilities. What they all have in common is that they will have met the rigorous criteria set out by the awarding bodies, and will have been judged capable of assessing the workplace competence of candidates.

••

Assessment centres undertake the task of determining whether and when candidates are competent and therefore ready for S/NVQ awards.

••

To summarize:

- **QCA and SQA** develop and administer the S/NVQ system and validate awards in England, Wales and Northern Ireland and in Scotland respectively.
- **Lead bodies,** or standard-setting bodies, develop and maintain written standards of competence and ensure that they are relevant in the workplace. The Information and Library Services Lead Body is responsible for our employment sector.
- **Awarding bodies** approve and oversee the organizations that assess candidates' competence, maintaining rigorous quality control procedures. At the end of the process, they award S/NVQs and issue certificates. At present, the awarding bodies for ILS are OCR and the Edexcel Foundation for England, Wales and Northern Ireland and SQA for Scotland.
- **Assessment centres** employ the staff who actually assess the competence of S/NVQ candidates. They are approved by an awarding body and have to satisfy rigorous criteria. They can be companies, local authorities or consortia of small organizations.

The individuals

The people involved in gaining and awarding S/NVQs have very clearly defined roles. This is not simply a matter of bureaucratic convenience – it is part of the process of ensuring consistency and uniformity across the whole S/NVQ system.

The candidate

The most important person is the **candidate** – you, perhaps. The S/NVQ system puts great emphasis on self-development and self-responsibility, and expects candidates to manage their own progress towards their qualifications (although, of course, not without support!). Candidates for ILS S/NVQs will include all sorts of people – employees, self-employed and voluntary workers, and even, under certain circumstances, students and those who are unemployed. All of these candidates will need to demonstrate their competence in different ways, bringing forward different kinds of evidence.

The system therefore has relatively few prescriptive requirements, stating what candidates must or must not do. If you are a candidate, it is up to you to read and understand the standards, up to you to judge what you can already do and where you need additional training or experience – and up to you to assemble evidence and seek opportunities to have it assessed. Acquiring your S/NVQ is a process that will be driven by you – there won't be any outsiders imposing timetables or instructing you what to do next. That may sound alarming – but it means that when you have finally gained your S/NVQ it will be your achievement alone, and no-one else's!

The candidate's role is to:

- take responsibility;
- identify existing areas of competence and sources of evidence;
- identify areas where training or additional experience is needed;
- negotiate learning opportunities and a personal development plan – on or off the job;
- develop and agree an assessment plan;
- collect and organize evidence;

- review evidence against the standards, checking that it is valid and sufficient;
- review progress.

••

Candidates are the most important people of all. They take responsibility for their own progress and development, and collect and organize the evidence which will lead to their being assessed as competent according to the national standards.

••

The assessor

Your **assessor** is the person appointed by your assessment centre to review the evidence of competence that you produce and judge whether it satisfies the requirements set out in the ILS standards. If you are in employment and your organization is an assessment centre, your assessor might well be your line manager. Equally, the role might be filled by an experienced colleague or a trainer – or even someone from another organization. But whoever your assessor is, there will be two conditions that will have been fulfilled:

- it will be someone with sufficient skills and knowledge within your area of work to assess your competence;
- it will be someone who has been trained in S/NVQ assessment.

It will also usually be someone with whom you have sufficient regular contact to enable you to get continuous feedback and encouragement.

The second condition – training in assessment – is not an empty requirement. Assessors in ILS S/NVQs will all be trained up to a standard which is itself defined as part of another sector's S/NVQs – the ones belonging to the Training and Development sector. They will be expected to gather evidence of competence in practical assessment sufficient to gain credits in two crucial S/NVQ Units which relate to assessing performance. So if you are planning to commit a great deal of time and effort to gaining an ILS S/NVQ, you will be able to reflect that your assessor is going to have to demonstrate an equal commitment, and will be expected to go through many of the same processes and procedures.

Assessor's role

The assessor's role is to:

- interpret the standards;
- introduce candidates to the assessment procedure and ensure that they understand their own roles and responsibilities;
- identify opportunities for candidates to collect evidence and demonstrate competence;
- negotiate assessment plans with candidates;
- judge candidates' evidence against the standards, checking that it is valid, current and sufficient;
- make objective assessment decisions and give candidates regular feedback;
- identify gaps in candidates' achievements and experience, and provide feedback;
- ensure fairness and equality of opportunity within the assessment process;
- maintain a record of candidates' progress and achievements, and sign off the official statements of achievement;
- meet regularly with other people in the S/NVQ assessment system to ensure consistency;
- attain and maintain competence in assessment, and work towards the relevant S/NVQ Units.

●●●

Assessors review evidence of competence and –
when they judge that the criteria set out in the
national standards have been met – sign off
candidates' achievements as part of the process
of gaining Unit certification.

●●●

Mentors, advisers or tutors

These terms are used to refer to people who can provide support, advice and counsel to candidates. They are not official roles within the S/NVQ system, but the words are very commonly used, and many employers and assessment centres set up an informal support network. The three terms are used almost interchangeably and there is no point in trying to make a distinction between them. I shall use the term **mentor.**

A mentor will generally be someone with knowledge and experience of the S/NVQ procedures who can help you make decisions about your personal development plan, and will be able to offer guidance during the process of selecting and organizing evidence. Quite often mentors are senior colleagues or managers who work closely with their candidates and who can authenticate, or even occasionally provide, evidence which candidates can put forward for assessment. Sometimes, on the other hand, they are trainers or teachers in another part of the organization – in which case their role is much more that of a neutral and objective adviser. Occasionally, especially in small organizations, the mentor's role will be undertaken by the assessor. The important thing from the candidate's point of view is that they provide support, encouragement and advice.

Mentor's role

A mentor's role is to:

- offer candidates support and encouragement;
- help candidates identify valid evidence, and suggest alternative or additional sources of material which can be put forward for assessment;
- assist and advise candidates in the presentation of evidence;
- help candidates in drawing up and negotiating their personal development plans.

....

Mentors offer candidates support and advice, and may become involved in their training or development plans. Their role is informal – they are not part of the official S/NVQ structure.

....

The verifiers

You will have seen from the first half of this chapter that S/NVQs are not assessed centrally, but in a large number of different and dispersed assessment centres. This means that there has to be a system to make sure that S/NVQs do not vary from centre to centre – which is where the **verifiers** come in. They play a very important role in ensuring that the S/NVQ system operates consistently and fairly across the country, and that S/NVQs gained in different centres are being assessed and awarded in ways that meet the national standards.

Verifiers are of two types – *internal* and *external*.

Internal verifiers

Every assessment centre will have at least one **internal verifier** for the ILS S/NVQs being offered, who is responsible for coordinating the systems and arrangements for delivering the qualification or qualifications, and also for ensuring that the centre's quality assurance mechanisms operate properly. The internal verifier oversees assessors and liaises with the awarding body, to make sure that the system runs smoothly and that Unit S/NVQ credits are not awarded for work which does not meet the national standards. (In some large centres the coordinating role and the quality assurance role are separated, and there may be someone called a *programme* or *centre coordinator*.)

Like assessors, internal verifiers of ILS S/NVQs have to meet certain conditions:

- they have to have the authority and responsibility to carry out the role of coordination and quality assurance. This means that they will usually be comparatively senior people;
- they have to have enough knowledge and experience of information and library services to make judgements about the assessment process and the performance of assessors;
- they have to be trained in S/NVQ assessment and verification, and should preferably have been trained in assessment as well.

Once again, the last requirement is not an empty one. Internal verifiers should ideally be trained to the standards set out in the Training and Development S/NVQ Units for assessors – but in addition they have to have or to be working towards an additional Unit which relates to verification.

Most of the internal verifier's role involves dealing with assessors – you as a candidate may see very little of this particular person in the system. Nevertheless, there are a number of aspects of the role that will have a direct impact on you. Among other things, the internal verifier is responsible for ensuring that:

- your assessor is properly trained and has access to any necessary support and advice;

- you are given a comprehensive and satisfactory induction to the centre's programme;
- your achievements in demonstrating competence are accurately recorded;
- you are given appropriate opportunities (as agreed in your development plan) to develop competence in areas relevant to your chosen qualification;
- you have access to a satisfactory and fair appeals procedure.

You will see from this that the internal verifier acts as a kind of referee, ensuring that the centre's systems operate as they should, and that all candidates have access to the information and facilities they need.

External verifier

Outside the assessment centre, the internal verifier's main point of liaison is with the **external verifier,** who is appointed by the awarding body, and is responsible for assessing the performance of the assessment centre, ensuring that its systems and procedures are fair and consistent, and that it is operating in accordance with the national standards. External verifiers are not members of the staff of the centres they oversee, but they visit regularly, meeting with both assessors and trainers. As well as looking at procedures, they sample and monitor candidates' evidence, checking that assessments have been carried out satisfactorily – and report back to the awarding body. Because they oversee a number of different centres, they are in a good position to offer advice and guidance, and also to disseminate good practice. They provide the all-important link that connects each individual candidate, working through one particular assessment centre, with the awarding body and the national S/NVQ system as a whole.

••

Verifiers act as referees, ensuring that the
assessment centre's procedures operate fairly,
and that assessments are being made according
to the criteria set out in the national standards.
Internal verifiers operate within an assessment
centre and are part of it; external verifiers are
appointed by the awarding body.

••

Summary of individuals

- **Candidates** are the most important people of all. They take responsibility for their own progress and development, and collect and organize the evidence which will lead to their being assessed as competent according to the national standards.
- **Assessors** work with candidates to develop evidence of competence. They review it and – when they judge that the criteria set out in the national standards have been met – sign off candidates' achievements as part of the process of gaining Unit certification.
- **Mentors** offer candidates support and advice, and may become involved in their training or development plans. Their role is informal – they are not part of the official S/NVQ structure.
- **Verifiers** act as referees, ensuring that the assessment centre's procedures operate fairly, and that assessments are being made according to the criteria set out in the national standards. **Internal** verifiers operate within an assessment centre and are part of it. **External** verifiers are appointed by the awarding body, and act as a link between individual centres and the national system.

In this chapter we have looked at the roles of the different organizations and individuals that go to make up the S/NVQ system. In the next chapter we will be concerned with the standards that have been developed, and which the system is designed to maintain and apply.

3 How to read an S/NVQ standard

In this chapter we will look at how the S/NVQ system defines competence, and therefore what it expects candidates to be able to do. You will learn how to 'read' the S/NVQ standards, and therefore how to determine what evidence of competence you will need to produce.

Introduction

Anyone seeking to gain an S/NVQ (or part of an S/NVQ) in Information and Library Services will be measured against a set of national standards, which break the ILS sector down into job areas and then define the types of competence required in each area. Each candidate registering for an S/NVQ should receive a copy of a document known as the **Cumulative Assessment Record (CAR)** or **Candidate Assessment Log (CAL)**, which contains the set of standards for the S/NVQ in question. In addition, each assessment centre may have a copy of a larger document, often called the **scheme book**, which contains a full set of standards for all the ILS S/NVQs. These documents are important, because they define what is expected of you as you pass through the S/NVQ process. It is therefore worth investing some time in getting to know the standards and understanding how they are presented and what they mean. This chapter should help you with that.

Units of Competence

S/NVQs are made up of modules called **Units of Competence**, which are in effect the building-blocks of the system. As we will see shortly, Units of Competence (or 'Units' for short) are the point at which you will receive S/NVQ credits. Units consist of a number of **standards**, and in order to gain credit for a Unit, you have to show that you are competent in each of the standards within it. (Standards are sometimes referred to as **elements** or **outcomes**.) When you have satisfied an assessor that you have met all the standards in a Unit, you will receive a certificate recognising your competence in that Unit. When you have demonstrated your competence in a specified set of Units, you will have acquired an S/NVQ. This system applies irrespective of the level of the S/NVQ, although higher-level S/NVQs require candidates to complete more Units. However, you don't have to proceed to a full S/NVQ if you don't want to. Single Units, or groups of Units that fall short of a full S/NVQ, have a perfectly acceptable and transferable value as mini-qualifications in their own right. Although a Unit can stand alone as a way of showing that you have met a standard of competence in a defined area, a single standard can't. That is why Units are the basic S/NVQ building-blocks.

In your CAR or CAL and in the Scheme Book you will find the Units grouped together into S/NVQs. Each S/NVQ consists of between six and twelve Units (depending on its level), covering a range of different skills and kinds of competence. Some of these Units are **mandatory** or **core** (that is, all candidates have to demonstrate competence in them in order to gain a full S/NVQ), and some are **optional** (that is, candidates wanting a full S/NVQ must complete a specified number, but can choose which ones to do).

• •

S/NVQs are made up of a set number of Units of Competence, which in turn contain a number of standards. Some Units are mandatory and some are optional.

• •

Reading a standard

Let us try to understand this structure by looking at a specific S/NVQ. There is an S/NVQ available in Information and Library Services at Level 3. It is made up of four mandatory, or core, Units and 15 optional Units. In order to gain the full S/NVQ, you would have to demonstrate competence in all of the four core Units and a further four of the optional Units – a total of eight Units in all. Figure 3.1 on page 36 shows this structure, breaking the S/NVQ down into its Units, and showing how the optional Units can be chosen to suit different candidates who approach the S/NVQ from different areas of experience.

One of the core Units of this S/NVQ has the title *Provide information and material to users*. The Unit contains three standards. They are *Retrieve information and material, Obtain information and material from external providers* and *Deliver information and material to user*. This means that candidates will have to show that they are competent at performing the tasks specified in these three standards before they can gain a credit for the Unit. You will find a full definition of this Unit in Figure 3.2 on page 37.

Information and Library Services S/NVQ: Level 3

Mandatory Units
Provide information and material to user
Identify information required by user
Solve problems on behalf of customers
Manage oneself

Optional Units

Option Group 1: Organizing Information
Organize material to preserve information
Index information
Create new information and material
Design and produce spreadsheets
Control the use of electronic communication

Option Group 2: User Services
Provide displays
Maintain a supportive environment for users
Evaluate and monitor the receipt of payments from customers for
    the purchase of goods and services
Provide induction and orientation activities for users
Enable clients to access and use information
Collect and process information for use with clients
Store and display information and material
Support users of the IT solution

Option Group 3: Supervising activities
Support the effective use of resources
Maintain activities to meet requirements
Create effective working relationships
Assess candidate performance
Assess candidate using differing sources of evidence

**Candidates must achieve the mandatory units and four optional
units, including one from each Option Group.**

Figure 3.1 *The Units that comprise an S/NVQ*

Unit IL3/1 Provide information and material to users
All candidates for the level 3 NVQ/SVQ in Information and Library Services must achieve this unit. You
- retrieve information and material from the correct location
- direct and help users to access information and material
- obtain information and material from an appropriate provider
- check that information and material meets the user's requirements
- prepare and give information and material to the user

There are three standards:
IL3/1.1 Retrieve information and material
IL3/1.2 Obtain information and material from external providers
IL3/1.3 Deliver information and material to user

KEY WORDS
Certain Key Words are listed and defined at the end of this Unit. You should use these to clarify the meaning of these terms in the standards. The Key Words are: **appropriate; material**

KEY SKILLS
If you achieve this unit, you will also achieve the following Key Skills:
Communication Level 3: Element 3.1 Take part in discussions; Element 3.2 Produce written material; Element 3.4 Read and respond to written materials.
Working With Others Level 3: Element 3.1 Identify collective goals and responsibilities; Element 3.2 Work to collective goals.

Figure 3.2 *The full definition of a Unit*

Quite clearly, then, it is very important to understand exactly what it is that you have to be able to do in order to demonstrate that you are competent at the work specified in a standard. You have to be able to read and understand the standard specification. In the rest of this chapter we will look in detail at how a standard is described and how the different parts of the description should be interpreted.

The standard we are going to look at is *Obtain information and material from external providers*, which is all to do with obtaining information or material from a source outside your own library or information unit. You will find a full definition of the standard in Figure 3.3 on pages 38–9.

Unit

IL3/1 PROVIDE INFORMATION AND MATERIAL TO USERS

You show that you can

IL3/1.2 Obtain information and material from external providers

So, you show that you . . .

1   request information and material from an appropriate provider
2   where the information and material has not arrived by the time it is needed by the user, take immediate follow-up action
3   check that the information and material is clear, complete and meets the user's needs, and take follow-up action with the provider where required
4   comply with any conditions imposed by the provider

You understand

What

K1 providers are available to the organization and their conditions of engagement
K2 conditions may be imposed by the provider, including copyright restrictions, confidentiality, preservation, return dates and fees payable
K3 issues arise from provider's conditions, and how to deal with these
K4 action to take when information does not meet the user's needs or is not available in time

How

K5 to identify appropriate providers
K6 to check that material is clean, complete and in a suitable for-mat

Figure 3.3 *The full definition of a standard*

Performance Evidence

To achieve the standard, you produce evidence from your work that you can obtain information and material from external providers consistently, over a period of time. Your assessor will observe you on at least one occasion.

You show, in your performance, that

R1 you can obtain at least one of the following types of information
• oral
• written
• electronic

Collecting the Evidence

1 If your performance evidence does not cover all of the evidence specified in R1, you must show your assessor that you under-stand these aspects of the standard. You can do this by using one of the following:
•   answering questions out to you by your assessor
•   showing how you have dealt with these aspects on (recent) earlier occasions

You should discuss this when planning your assessment with your assessor.

2 External providers may be other departments in-house or exter-nal to your organisation.

Also please read the Notes. [These are reproduced as Appendix 1]

Figure 3.3 *Continued*

Understanding the functions of the Unit

The first thing you must do in order to understand the standard is to understand the functions of the Unit of which it forms part. In the case of our standard, 'obtaining information and material from external providers' is placed in the context of a Unit which is all to do with 'providing information or material to users' (see Figure 3.2 on page 37). The first part of the definition of the Unit tells you exactly what is meant by 'provide information and material to users'. It states that you should be able to:

- retrieve information and material from the correct location;
- direct and help users to access information and material;
- obtain information and material from an appropriate provider;
- check that information and material meets the user's requirements; and
- prepare and give information and material to the user.

All of the standards in the Unit are part of these functions. In other words, you are not being asked to show that you can obtain any old information from any old source and for any old reason. To be relevant, your activities to do with obtaining information have to be purposive, and linked to a role in retrieving, assessing and providing information or material as part of a service to users.

••

Locating your standard in the Unit of which it is part, and understanding the purpose of the Unit as a whole, is essential if you are to understand what the activity described by the standard is, and why it is important.

••

Title

The next part of the standard you should look at is the Title. This is a brief statement explaining what the standard is about, beginning with the phrase 'You should show that you can . . .'. In the case of the standard we are looking at, you 'should show that you can obtain information and material from external providers'. Think about these words carefully, because they define exactly what the standard is about and what is required of you. All of the sections of the definition which follow are part of that requirement. Everything that you do in order to gain credit for this standard should be seen as part of a process of showing that you are competent at obtaining information or material from external provider.

••

Understanding the title of your standard will help you interpret the rest of the standard definition, and will assist you in deciding what evidence of competence to offer.

••

Performance criteria

After you have thought about the standard's title, you should go on to the first section, which is a series of statements beginning with the phrase 'So, you show that you . . .' – see Figure 3.3. These statements (which are usually referred to as **performance criteria**) define what it is you are expected to do in order to show that you are competent at the task defined in the standard title. If you are to be considered competent at obtaining information from external sources, you have to be able to go through the following processes (although, of course, not necessarily in any particular order):

- request the information and material from an appropriate provider (criterion 1);
- where the information and material does not arrive by the time it is needed by the user, take immediate follow-up action (criterion 2);
- check that the information and material is clear, complete and meets the user's needs, and take follow-up action with the provider where required (criterion 3);
- comply with any conditions imposed by the provider (criterion 4).

You should notice that these criteria do not refer to the specific physical, administrative or computer procedures involved. Most of them refer to matters of judgement. If your job required you to do a lot of interlibrary loans or computer searches yourself, then you would seek credit for this standard on the basis of your decisions about what to obtain and how to do it. However, it would not be sufficient simply to show that you were able to follow set procedures. You would also have to show that you can identify when something is going wrong, and what to do about it. There are times when what you have requested fails to arrive, or turns out to be unsuitable for the user's needs. You would be expected to show that you can exercise your judgement and make sensible decisions on these and similar matters. In other words, being competent in the area of 'obtaining information and material' means more than just being handy with the ILL forms – it means understanding the processes involved and knowing what action to take in particular circumstances.

You should also notice that there is nothing in the definition of the standard about *how* you should set about your tasks. There is nothing, for example, prohibiting the use of expensive databases or demanding that you use a particular request service. That is because the standard represents a general standard of competence which can be applied in all sorts of different libraries and information units. It is not prescribing a particular method or approach to obtaining information because to do that would make the standard less universal in its application – there would inevitably be circumstances in which that method would be inappropriate.

···

The standard sets out exactly what it is you are expected to do in order to demonstrate competence, by means of a series of statements usually called 'performance criteria'.

···

The knowledge requirements

It is quite obviously impossible to be competent at any task without having some degree of understanding of the ideas, theories or principles which underlie what you are doing. Establishing your knowledge and understanding of the tasks which you perform is the part of the S/NVQ system which acknowledges the need for this abstract or intellectual component of competence. It is sometimes referred to as **Underpinning Knowledge and Understanding** or **UKU**.

Knowledge and understanding requirements are usually presented in the form of statements introduced by the phrase 'You understand . . .'. In the case of the standard we are looking at, there are six 'understanding' requirements, numbered K1 to K6 as shown in Figure 3.3 on pages 38–9 (the 'K' stands for 'Knowledge'). The first requirement is that you should understand

What providers are available to the organisation, and their conditions of engagement.

Obtaining information or material does not take place in a vacuum. It is undertaken within an organization that has certain relationships – either informal agreements or detailed contracts – with other organizations. You cannot be considered competent at performing those tasks unless you have acquired, and can show you have acquired, an understanding of which providers you may use, and on what terms.

The second 'knowledge' requirement is that you should understand

> What conditions may be imposed by the provider, including copyright restrictions, confidentiality, preservation, return dates and fees payable.

Criterion 4 of the performance criteria is concerned with complying with any conditions imposed by the provider. Evidently, you cannot comply with those conditions if you do not understand what they are. So you cannot be considered competent in the tasks concerned with obtaining information unless you can show you understand, for example, that copyright law may have an effect on your decisions – and that it may be necessary to obtain permission before photocopying a document or copying a downloaded file on to a floppy disk.

The third 'knowledge' requirement is that you should understand

> What issues arise from the provider's conditions, and how to deal with these.

Sometimes the conditions imposed by providers can give rise to ethical issues, and you have to show that you understand these and can take appropriate action. For example, in a situation where there was a conflict between a user's need for confidentiality and an information provider's requirement that all loans be logged and reported, you would have to show first, that you understood the issue and second, that you could take the matter forward by explanation, negotiation or referral to a higher authority. Do note, however, that this 'knowledge' requirement does not mean that you have to be an expert in all aspects of copyright and information provision law – only that you must understand the kinds of implications it may have for your decisions and subsequent actions.

The 'knowledge' requirements continue in a similar vein, with a total of six in the standard we are examining. In each case, there is a clear relationship between what you are required to do (as set out in the performance criteria) and what you are required to know and understand. The close relationship between competent performance on the one hand, and knowledge and understanding on the other, is clearly described in the standard in terms of what you have to demonstrate in order to be judged competent.

••

The 'knowledge' requirements (sometimes called Underpinning Knowledge and Understanding) set out the areas of theoretical or intellectual understanding which are necessary if the tasks defined in the standard are to be performed competently.

••

Simple instructions and clear guidance

If you have been reading the wording of the standard with care (refer back to Figure 3.3), you will have noticed something about the way in which the requirements are expressed. You can, in effect, read the first two sections as three simple sentences – like this:

You show that you can obtain information and material from external providers.

So, you show that you [can do each of four different things]. You understand [each of six different aspects of the work in question].

These sentences are, quite simply, the instructions you need to follow if you want to demonstrate your competence in the case of this particular standard. Although they contain a lot of detail and may seem complicated when you first approach them, they are actually very straightforward, giving simple instructions and clear guidance. This is now the normal way in which all S/NVQ standards are written.

That brings us to the end of the part of the standard definition which sets out the required standards of competence. You will see from Figure 3.3 that there are two more parts to the standard definition, which are called **Performance evidence** and **Collecting the evidence**. You will find these discussed at the end of the next chapter. But at this point, let us summarise what has been said so far about the different parts of a standard definition.

The standard: a summary

UNIT

This defines the context of the standard. The Unit describes the segment or area of activity of which the standard is part, and lists the tasks or functions involved in that activity. Locating a standard in the Unit of which it is part, and understanding the purpose of the Unit as a whole, is essential if you are to understand what the purpose of the standard's activity is and why it is important.

Standard title

This is a statement which begins 'You show that you can . . .', and which briefly sets out what you have to do in order to meet the standard. Careful consideration of the title will help you interpret the rest of the standard definition, and will assist you in deciding what evidence of competence to offer.

Performance criteria

These are expressed as a statement which begins 'So, you show that you . . .'. They break down the type of work defined in the standard title, and set out exactly what it is that you are expected to do in order to demonstrate competence and meet the standard.

Knowledge and understandng

Competence in information and library work requires the application of a certain level of knowledge. This section of a standard (introduced by the phrase 'you understand') sets out the areas of theoretical or intellectual understanding which are necessary if the tasks defined in the standard are to be performed competently.

In this chapter we have taken a close look at the published standards, using one standard as an example, and seen how they define what is expected of S/NVQ candidates. In the next chapter we will find out how you can set about demonstrating that your own performance meets the standards.

4 Evidence and how it is assessed

This chapter is about the evidence that you have to present in order to demonstrate your competence. You will find out what kinds of evidence are acceptable and how you can best choose your material so that it makes your case clearly and effectively.

The nature of evidence

S/NVQs are not awarded on the basis of tests or examinations. Instead, candidates are expected to produce evidence which demonstrates that their work conforms to the national standards. This evidence will always be directly work-related. However, there are all sorts of ways in which work-related evidence can be gathered and presented, and it is important to understand the different categories and types of evidence, because it will make it easier for you to plan and prepare.

Performance evidence

The most important category of evidence is referred to as **performance evidence**, because it derives directly from your performance at work. Broadly speaking, there are two types of performance evidence – evidence of product and evidence of process. **Product evidence** is related to the direct output of work you have done – it is evidence of the end result of your work – it will usually be something tangible. **Process evidence**, on the other hand, involves looking at how you work, watching what you are doing in your workplace and comparing what you do with the standards of competence. In other words, someone at some stage will observe you working, and will make notes about how you perform. Those notes, in whatever form they are put together, will form the evidence.

••
Performance evidence is derived directly from
your work. It can be
• process evidence
• product evidence.
••

Product evidence

Product evidence can be anything which you have produced or completed or contributed towards which demonstrates that your work meets the criteria set out in the standards. It might be a printout of a computer search you have done, or photographs of a display you have mounted, or it might take the form of letters, reports and memos you have written or with which you have been involved. Some pieces of documentary evidence will self-evidently be your work, some may need to be authenticated to indicate your involvement – for example, if you have drawn a guide map of your library, a note from your manager might be required to show that it was indeed your work. You will probably find that most of the evidence you wish to collect will be product evidence of one sort or another.

••

Product evidence is the direct output of work you
have done, and is one form of performance
evidence.

••

Process evidence

Process evidence is usually generated by observation, which
can be the quickest, and sometimes the clearest, way of assessing someone's performance. An assessor can see both the
input to a task (the material to be worked with, for example,
or the enquiry to be answered) and the output (the processed
result, or the answer), and can look at how the candidate has
dealt with the task in a particular set of circumstances – and
ask questions if needs be. The assessor will normally have
developed or be working from a checklist. Observation of this
kind is well-suited to assessing practical skills – like those
involved in routine cataloguing, or processing books for issue.

   However, observation is a very much less satisfactory
method when it comes to assessing skills which have a
significant thinking or conceptual element, because the
assessor cannot see the reasoning or reflection that has
led the candidate to choose one course of action rather
than another. For this reason, other forms of evidence
might be required in addition to the observation.

••

Process evidence involves your assessor looking
at how you work. It is another form of performance
evidence.

••

Supplementary evidence

Most of what you put into your portfolio will be performance evidence deriving directly from work you do as part of your present job or have done in the past. However, there may be circumstances in which performance evidence is difficult to obtain – for example, because your normal job does not cover one of the situations specified in the standard. In these cases you can present what is known as **supplementary evidence**. This is evidence derived from situations outside your normal work routine – for example, from questioning by your assessor, or from off-the-job testing. Supplementary evidence is most commonly used to support demonstration of your knowledge and understanding, or to show that evidence which is more than three years old is still currently valid.

....

Supplementary evidence is obtained by questioning or testing, and is used to supplement performance evidence in cases where the latter is unavailable.

....

There are no particular restrictions on the form that evidence takes. Your portfolio can include notes, letters, photographs, computer programs – even tape or video recordings. Nor does the evidence have to derive from your present job – you can use documents from previous jobs if you wish, although, as a general rule, if the evidence is more than three years old you will have to show that you have kept your competence up to date. Three things matter, however. The first is that the evidence relates *closely* to the standards and evidence requirements. The second is that each piece, or sample, of evidence addresses *all* the performance criteria in the standard to which it relates. The third is that the evidence you present makes it clear what your role has been – it must be sufficient to demonstrate *your own* performance.

∙∙∙

Evidence
- must relate to all the performance criteria in a standard
- must be sufficient to demonstrate your performance
- can be presented in any practicable form
- does not necessarily have to be from your present job
- if more than three years old, must be shown to be still current

∙∙∙

The assessment of evidence

As we have seen, it is your assessor who decides whether your evidence demonstrates competence or not. Assessors, however, do not work in a vacuum. The standards which provide you with guidance as to what evidence is required, and what it has to show, also provide assessors with guidance as to what to look for.

If you turn back to the standard definition we looked at in detail in Chapter 3 (Figure 3.3 on pages 38–9), you will see a section headed 'Performance Evidence', which tells you what your evidence must show, and specifies any evidence requirements. You will also see a section headed 'Collecting the Evidence' which gives you some guidelines about how to make sure that your evidence covers the full range of circumstances required by the standard.

Although the wording of these sections is aimed at you, the candidate, it applies just as much to your assessor. Both of you are working from the same standard — you in collecting evidence and your assessor in assessing it. This means that you are both given the same guidance. Provided that you read the standard carefully and plan how you are going to collect evidence — and provided that you discuss your plans with your assessor — you should not encounter any problems over whether particular evidence is sufficient, relevant or acceptable.

In addition to the guidance on evidence that forms part of the standard, there are some general notes which are intended to help assessors decide what kind of evidence, and how much, is appropriate. These notes apply to the assessment of all standards, and are reproduced as Appendix 1 on pages 100–14.

Types of evidence

Evidence may take many forms. Remember, however, that what is important about evidence is not its form but what it demonstrates. Each piece of evidence should show that your performance meets all the criteria set out in the standard.

Performance evidence may be provided by:

- *Work products.* Common examples of work products include written notes, file notes, memos, letters, requisition or ILL documents, reports to users. However, these are only examples — if appropriate, you could, for example, submit a downloaded search on a computer disk, or even a short video.
- *Observation.* Your assessor may be required to gather evidence by observing you while you are engaged in an

activity which demonstrates that you can meet the performance criteria.

- *Personal report of actual work situations.* You can include in your portfolio accounts of your work which you have written yourself – although, clearly, they will need to be authenticated to ensure that they are accurate!
- *Witness reports from colleagues, users or providers.* You can also include accounts by those who work with you, or even users to whom you supply information. Witness reports from your manager are particularly useful, and are sometimes required.

Supplementary evidence may be provided by:

- *Questioning, in areas of activity where no performance evidence is provided.* Your assessor can establish whether you can apply your skills in some of the situations set out in the standard by asking questions. However, there is always a minimum number of situations for which you *must* submit performance evidence.
- *Verbal or written tests of knowledge and understanding, where this cannot be demonstrated through performance evidence.* Your assessor can test your knowledge and understanding of matters which are not easily demonstrated directly by performance – for example, copyright or data protection regulations.

The standards do not specify what form evidence should take – only what it should demonstrate. Before deciding what evidence to collect, you should discuss with your assessor how you can best demonstrate that your performance meets the standards. Then you should make sure that all your evidence is *efficient* – that is, that every piece of evidence shows clearly and indisputably what it is supposed to show.

••

Performance evidence may be provided by:
• work products
• observation
• personal reports
• witness reports.
Supplementary evidence may be provided by:
• questioning
• verbal or written tests.

••

Evidence requirements
You will recall that your evidence has to show that you meet all the performance criteria for every standard before you can gain credit for an S/NVQ Unit – and that you can apply your competence in a range of situations. Evidence has to be:

• *sufficient* – it has to cover enough of the ground
• *current* – it has to show that your skills are still relevant
• *in an acceptable context* – it has to be work-related.

Let us look at these three aspects in turn.

Sufficiency of evidence
Your evidence has to be *sufficient* to show that you are competent at the work specified in the standard, and that your competence could be transferred to a different work environment. That means that you have to demonstrate that you can meet all the performance criteria set out in the standard, and do so in a range of different situations

(although, of course, you are bound to be more familiar with some situations than others).

In order for your evidence to be sufficient, therefore, it must show that you can meet the requirements of the standard, and that you can do so in a range of different circumstances. Requirements about the nature and sufficiency of evidence are set out in the section headed 'Performance Evidence'. These requirements are sometimes called **evidence indicators.** If you turn back to the standard in Figure 3.3 (pages 38–9), you will see that the 'Performance Evidence' section includes a requirement that your assessor should observe you on at least one occasion, i.e. there is a requirement for at least one piece of observation evidence. In this section you will also find a statement setting out the range of different situations your evidence should cover. In the case of this standard, as you can see, it should cover three types of information: oral, written and electronic. This 'Performance Evidence' section therefore tells you what kind of evidence you must show, and what range of situations it should cover. (You may have noticed that the statement of the range of situations your evidence should cover is numbered R1. The 'R' stands for 'Range' – these statements are sometimes called **range statements.**)

Collecting the evidence

It is normal for standards to specify a minimum number of situations which must be covered by direct performance evidence. In the standard we have been looking at, you have to provide direct performance evidence to show that you can obtain only one of the three types of information specified in R1. However, the fact that a minimum number of situations is specified does not mean that you can avoid producing evidence about the whole range. The next section of the standard, states that if your performance evidence does not cover all three of these situations, then you must still show your assessor that you understand how to deal with any situations not covered – and it goes on to suggest how you could do this. This section, 'Collecting the Evidence', therefore, is used to give you additional information about what supplementary evidence is suggested or required to clarify or supplement your performance evidence (see Figure 3.3).

Let us illustrate this with an example. Suppose that you normally obtain only written and printed material for users – say, by working on interlibrary loans. You will be able to produce plenty of direct evidence from your work showing that you can obtain written information, but none that you can obtain oral or electronic information. In this case you will have to show that you understand how to meet the performance criteria when obtaining oral or electronic information by producing supplementary evidence. To gather this evidence, you will probably use one of the ways set out in the section headed 'Collecting the Evidence'. When you have done this, you will have shown that you can meet the standard required in the full range of situations specified, even though your direct work experience relates to only one of the situations.

The 'Collecting the Evidence' section is also used to explain the meaning of any important or ambiguous words or phrases. In the case of the standard in Figure 3.3, for example, it clarifies exactly what is meant by the words 'external providers'. In some standards, this section is quite lengthy, with many examples of evidence and suggestions about how to go about collecting it.

Obviously, in addition to showing that you can perform satisfactorily in the full range of situations set out in the standards, you must also show that you can perform consistently and over a period of time. Your evidence, therefore, will have to show that you have performed satisfactorily on more than one occasion. You could do this by producing several different pieces of performance evidence relating to different occasions. It is, however, often acceptable for you to produce performance evidence for one occasion and support it with statements from other people, such as your manager, testifying that you have performed similar tasks in the same way on other occasions.

Do note, however, that you should not submit more evidence than is necessary to demonstrate your competence. You do not get a 'better' S/NVQ by gathering a greater quantity of evidence – you merely make it more difficult to assess you!

••

Evidence must be sufficient. This means it must:
• cover a minimum number of areas of activity with performance evidence;
• cover all other areas with supplementary evidence;
• demonstrate consistency of performance.
Evidence, however, should not be excessive in quantity.

••

Currency of information

Competence involves keeping skills up to date. This means that your evidence has to be *current* – you have to demonstrate that your skills and knowledge can be applied in today's working environment. There is nothing to prevent you producing evidence which relates to work you have done in the past, but if you wish to submit anything which will be more than three years old at the time of assessment, then you have to provide supplementary evidence to show that you can transfer your competent performance into situations you would encounter today. The supplementary evidence could be produced by your assessor questioning you about how you would set about a similar task now, or in some circumstances it could involve a simulation, in which you work through a task set up specially for the purpose.

....

In order to be current evidence must be:
- less than three years old, or
- accompanied by supplementary evidence if more than three years old.

....

Context of criteria

Your evidence should be *work-related* – it should be generated in the context of a working environment (whether paid or voluntary), which will usually be your normal place and circumstances of work. However, it is possible that your normal work does not involve you in one of the situations set out in the 'Performance Evidence' section of the standard. In this situation, evidence can still be acceptable, even if it has been generated in a more artificial context – for example, from a test or a special project or even, exceptionally, from a simulation designed to enable you to demonstrate how you would perform.

The possibility of using special projects or tests is important, because it provides a way forward for candidates whose normal employment simply does not cover a sufficient variety of activities for them to be able to complete a Unit with evidence generated directly from work. It allows an assessor to accept evidence which comes out of activities which are not part of the candidate's normal work, such as projects which have been set specifically in order to test performance. Provided that the projects are realistically related to work, evidence produced in this way is acceptable as performance evidence, and can, therefore, contribute to the minimum requirements for evidence which we looked at earlier.

Simulation exercises

It is also possible for an assessor to set up a simulation to test a candidate's performance. Simulations should always be used with caution, and you will find that assessors will accept them only exceptionally, when there is no alternative. This is because a simulation is not real work, and competence, in the S/NVQ sense, relates always to performance in a real working environment. Nevertheless, there are circumstances in which some aspect of a standard simply cannot be assessed in any other way. In these cases, a carefully designed simulation will be the only way forward. Do note, however, that simulations will always be comparatively rare, will only be used when there is no alternative way of generating evidence, and will never form a large part of the assessment process.

You will find more information about the use of evidence derived from projects and simulations in the Assessment Guidance notes reproduced as Appendix 1.

••

Evidence must be from an acceptable context:
- usually, from the normal working environment;
- if necessary, from assignments, projects or transfers;
- exceptionally, from simulations.

••

Status of non-S/NVQ qualifications

Finally, before we leave the subject of evidence, let us deal briefly with the status within the S/NVQ system of other, non-S/NVQ, qualifications. Many people who work in the ILS sector already have vocational certificates (such as those issued by the City & Guilds of London Institute) – to say nothing of degrees and professional qualifications. These obviously have enormous value, and the skills and learning acquired will prove very important when it comes to assembling evidence. However, in the past, none of these qualifications was assessed with reference to any national ILS standards, and so there is no direct equivalence between one system and the other. This means that an existing non-S/NVQ library or information services qualification cannot be simply transferred into the S/NVQ system as a certain number of Unit credits. Nevertheless, there are two ways in which such a qualification can be an important part of your progress towards an S/NVQ. First, the training you received and the experience you gained will have enhanced your skills, and you will almost certainly find that you have performance evidence that demonstrates the additional competence you acquired. Second, the fact that you have covered a syllabus and were tested on it will prove very useful when it comes to bringing forward supplementary evidence, particularly concerning your knowledge and understanding. So, although you cannot transfer a previous qualification directly into S/NVQ credits, you will find that what you learned can be easily translated into S/NVQ evidence.

Evidence, as we have seen, can be generated in a lot of different ways, and is acceptable provided it meets the various requirements set out in the standards. In the next chapter we will look at how to organize evidence into a portfolio.

5 How to plan your portfolio

Evidence has to be organized and presented in a way that is as easy as possible to understand. This chapter makes some suggestions about how to set about it, based on some techniques widely used for S/NVQs.

Introduction

In order to gain an S/NVQ, or part of an S/NVQ, you have to assemble documentary and other evidence of your performance which demonstrates to an assessor that you are competent. The easiest and by far the most common way of doing this is to create what is referred to as a **portfolio**. A little later in this chapter we will see how to set about organizing a portfolio - but first, let us look at what you are going to need to put into it.

Contents of a portfolio

In the last chapter we looked at the criteria and methods of assessment in some detail, and we saw how performance is measured against precisely defined standards which have been drawn up with reference to the real work environment. It follows that any evidence put forward for assessment should be:

- directly related to the standard(s) being assessed
- clear, consistent and well-presented

- set in the context of your job
- not excessive in quantity.

With that in mind, let us look at what kind of material a successful portfolio might contain. The emphasis here is on the word 'might'. There are no formal or universal regulations here – the only requirement is that it should contain the evidence that the assessor needs in order to be satisfied that you meet the standards of competence.

However, you should remember that your portfolio is quite unlike an examination essay or assignment, which you will want to complete and then, probably, forget all about. It is something with a long-term, even permanent, value. Some of what you gather together in order to gain Units at Level 2 may well form part of your submission for a later Level 3 or 4 qualification. Furthermore, your portfolio is – or should be – an important personal document. It is, after all, a description and demonstration of your work-related skills and a summary of your achievements to date. If you think of it in those terms, and put into it as much care and attention as you can, you will produce a better submission, and one of which you can be proud.

You should also remember that the Units and qualifications you are being assessed for are in the area of library and information work. You will be seeking to demonstrate that you have certain competences in dealing with information. A well organized portfolio, containing well-selected evidence arranged in a clear and easily understood way, immediately says something important and relevant about its owner. After all, organizing information for easy retrieval is at the heart of what information work is all about!

Compiling a portfolio can take a long time. It may be that you can quickly put together evidence of competence in some or all of the standards and Units of an S/NVQ – in which case, go ahead. But sooner or later, as your career develops and as you seek to acquire a wider range of Units at higher levels, you will find that you have to develop new competences. This is where S/NVQs can help your personal and professional development, because they provide a structure within which the new skills can be sought and gained.

••

Your portfolio:
- must relate to the standard(s) being assessed;
- must relate to you, your work and your performance
- will be a permanent record of your achievements;
- should be well organized;
- will take time to compile.

••

Planning a portfolio

Your portfolio, if it is properly planned, will be a document which will help you manage your own training and career development as you progress through the S/NVQ system. So don't worry if the S/NVQ you have set your sights on contains elements where you do not yet feel yourself to be competent. Establish clear and realistic goals (in discussion with your employer, if you wish) and then incorporate them into the portfolio – and record when you have achieved them. Your career should be an interesting and dynamic process, always developing and changing – and so therefore should be the record of your skills and achievements.

Format for portfolio

There is no required format for a portfolio – but the commonest method is to use an ordinary ring binder, with a supplementary document case for any large charts or illustrations. And, as we have seen, there are no set requirements for what should be included or how the material should be arranged – but there are some conventions which you can use or adapt as you wish.

Most portfolios fall into three broad sections (which can, of course, be subdivided as much as you want). The three sections are:

- Introduction and background
- Planning and management
- Evidence

We will look at each of these sections in turn.

First portfolio section: introduction and background

The overall purpose of this section is to give your assessor (and any other people who see your portfolio, such as verifiers) the essential background information which will enable them to understand two things. First, they will need to know how you have organized the documentation, and where to find information they are looking for. Second, they will need to understand a bit about you, your background and the circumstances of your work. It doesn't matter how you achieve that purpose – but certain items are so nearly standard, and are so helpful to assessors, that you should think very carefully before omitting them. These items include:

- Title page
- Table of contents
- List of abbreviations and unusual terms
- Your curriculum vitae
- Your job description
- A profile of your organization

Title page

Remember that your portfolio will be seen by a number of people, most of whom will be dealing with many S/NVQ candidates. A title page will help them, at a glance, identify what the document is – so put on your name and the title of the S/NVQ. It may also be appropriate to include the name of the awarding body and that of your organization, particularly if you are being supported or sponsored.

Table of contents

Your portfolio will almost certainly be divided into sections, each with a different purpose and containing different types of documents. A table of contents is needed to help your assessor understand how the material has been organized, and how to locate the different elements of evidence and background information. It will also be helpful to you, because it will show you the structure of your portfolio at a glance and may help you identify any omissions, or items of information which might be more logically placed in another section.

List of abbreviations and unusual terms

We have all been irritated by books and articles that use acronyms, abbreviations and technical words without explaining them. Don't make the same mistake yourself! Your assessor will be very familiar with information work, both in broad terms and in detail, and will take some trouble to become conversant with your particular specialized area. But information work is very varied, and it would be unreasonable to expect every assessor to be an expert in every type of special library or every area of technical expertise. The courtesy of providing a guide to the abbreviations and unusual terms that are common in your area of work will certainly be appreciated. But again, the list will be helpful to you, because it will help you to be consistent and accurate in the way in which you use any specialized terms – and to ensure that you are using them because they are needed, and not as a sort of verbal smoke-screen to disguise uncertainty or lack of confidence.

....

- A title page identifies your portfolio and helps it look smart
- A contents page helps those who look at your portfolio to find what they are looking for
- A list of abbreviations and acronyms helps avoid misunderstandings and is a courtesy to your assessor

....

An outline curriculum vitae (CV)

The evidence of competence that you present will be yours and no-one else's, and it has to be seen in the context of your own experience and career development. If the evidence in your portfolio comes from different jobs, your assessor will find the CV useful as a way of gaining an overview of where you have worked; and your mentors and anyone else to whom you show your portfolio may use it to gain an impression of your experience and interests. You don't need to put in all the detail that would go into a full CV for, say, a job application, but you should include:

- your name and address;
- academic qualifications from school on;
- other qualifications and the names of any professional bodies of which you are a member;
- your work experience and employment history;
- your training and career development history – the important courses attended, with dates and other details;
- your leisure interests if they are relevant.

If you are compiling a CV for the first time, don't forget to keep it up-to-date – you never know when it may come in handy!

Your job description(s)

Just as the evidence you collect has to be seen in the context of you as a person, so it has to be seen in the context of your job. If you have a job description, it will set out your main responsibilities and duties. If you don't – either because you are not conventionally employed or because your organization does not provide one – then you should consider writing one for yourself, describing the purpose and key areas of your work. It may have no official status, but it will be a useful guide for your mentors and assessor. And remember that if you are presenting evidence relating to previous jobs you have held, you should include job descriptions for those as well.

A profile of your organization

Just as your evidence has to be understood in the context of your job, so your job has to be understood in the context of your employer's organization. You should therefore include a section to introduce the organization to those who are unfamiliar with it, and to explain your position and role within it. A brief account of the organization's history and structure may be useful, together with a more detailed account of the section or department within which you work. A mission statement or a list of organization or departmental aims and objectives is often helpful, and an account of the main goods or services supplied will clarify the role and purpose of a commercial firm. If other people in the organization have been associated with your efforts in compiling your portfolio – for example, a training officer or an S/NVQ mentor – then you may consider listing their names and job titles and providing an organization chart which makes clear the relationship between you and them. And once again, if you are presenting evidence relating to previous jobs you have held, you need to repeat the process for those earlier employers.

....

- An outline CV is useful to show where evidence has come from.
- Job descriptions indicate the context in which work has been done.
- Organization profiles explain the purpose for which work has been done.

....

Second portfolio section: planning and management

This is the section of the portfolio that you use both to plan your learning objectives and to manage and record your progress towards meeting those objectives. It is in this section that your portfolio can (and should) become more than a static exercise in demonstrating whether you possess certain skills, and turn into a valuable and important tool assisting your personal and professional self-development.

You can use this section to:

- record the standards of performance you need to achieve;
- establish and record what you need to learn;
- draw up a development plan, which you may need to agree with your employer;
- draw up an assessment plan, which you may need to agree with your assessor;
- assess and record your own progress.

Performance standards

When you register for an S/NVQ, you should receive a document called either a **Cumulative Assessment Record (CAR)**, or a **Candidate Assessment Log (CAL)**. Part of the CAR or CAL is a copy of the standards for all the Units that form part of your S/NVQ. It should be kept in the portfolio, where you can easily find it. Remember – your portfolio is intended to demonstrate that you are competent in relation to these specific standards. You will need to refer to them constantly, to check whether evidence is sufficient and complete. If you do not keep referring to them, you will find yourself gathering evidence which is inadequate and irrelevant.

....

Keep the performance standards handy. You will need to refer to them all the time.

....

Learning needs and goals

As you get to know the standards of performance that you are required to demonstrate in order to gain your S/NVQ, you will quickly realize that there are some areas where you are already competent, some areas where you are perhaps not yet fully competent, and some areas where you have little or no experience. You will need to record these strengths and weaknesses, because they indicate your learning needs and will form the basis of your plans for getting extra training or additional experience.

A good way of assessing your current level of competence against the standards is to draw up a chart on which you can record your own assessment of your level of competence against every performance criterion in every standard of the Units you are concerned with. Figure 5.1 (overleaf) shows what a self-assessment chart might look like. In each square in the 'performance criteria' columns you need to put a score – between 100% for fully competent and 0% for not yet competent at all. Then if you add all the scores for a standard together and divide by the number of performance criteria, you will

Unit or standard number	Unit or standard title	Performance Criteria								Score (0-100%)	
		1	2	3	4	5	6	7	8	Element	Unit
Score your competence on a scale of 0-100%						Date:					

Figure 5.1 *An example of a self-assessment chart*

have a percentage rating for that standard. You will find these scores a useful guide to the areas where you can feel confident, and those where you need additional experience.

••
Using the performance standards, assess your own competence at the very beginning – it will help you understand your own learning needs.
••

Development plan

When you have established the areas in which you feel that you are not yet fully competent, think about how you will get the additional experience or training you need. You might consider drawing up a development plan for yourself, with specific proposals and a timetable. You may need to agree all or part of your plan with your employer, particularly if you want to negotiate additional job experience or work-based training. However, do remember that experience gained outside paid employment can produce perfectly acceptable performance evidence – so jobs undertaken on a voluntary or unpaid basis can form part of your plan.

••
Draw up a development plan – it will help you meet your learning needs.
••

Assessment plan

There are no formal timetables associated with S/NVQ assessment – there are, for example, no set dates for you to submit your portfolio. This has the great advantage that it allows you to learn, progress and collect evidence at your own pace. However, may people find that without a timetable and some sort of deadline they are inclined to let self-development projects slip. For this reason, you may find it helpful to draw up an assessment plan, in which you set out the dates by which you propose to have different groups of evidence ready for assessment.

Your plan should be organized around the standards that you are preparing for assessment. The standards in which you feel that you are already fully competent can be presented early in the plan, and got out of the way, leaving you time to prepare for those you will find more difficult because you need extra experience or training. Make sure that your plan is realistic, particularly with regard to timing. A common mistake is to imagine you can gain competence in new areas quickly – you can't!

Clearly, your development plan and your assessment plan relate to each other very closely. And just as you may need to negotiate your development plan with your employer, so you should agree your assessment plan with your assessor. Your mentor, if you have one, will probably have some useful advice to offer as well.

....

Draw up an assessment plan – it will give you targets to aim for and help you discipline yourself.

....

Progress and self-assessment

We have already looked at a self-assessment chart (Figure 5.1) and seen how it can be used to determine areas of strength and weakness. The same chart can be used to record progress. If you complete a self-assessment at regular intervals – say, every three or six months, you will have a very helpful and interesting record of how your skills are evolving and your competence is growing.

Taken together, your development plan, your assessment plan and your self-assessment charts will form the basis of a good control system – to help you manage your development as you progress towards your S/NVQ.

Regular self-assessment, using the chart and referring always to the performance standards, will give you a valuable record of your progress.

Third portfolio section: evidence

Organizing evidence

A portfolio can become extremely complex (although the evidence seldom runs into more than one volume). It is very important, therefore, to give careful thought to its organization. As with so many things, the best system is probably the simplest.

Remember that a single piece of evidence – one document or diagram, for example – can refer to more than one standard. It is, therefore, a good idea to avoid organizing your evidence according to the standards it refers to, because it will create the need for a complex system of cross-reference. Most assessors will recommend that you keep all the evidence in the portfolio in a single sequence, with every item identified by a running number (sometimes called a **Reference Identifier**). Then, when you want to draw attention to a particular item, you can simply refer to it by number. The process of identifying pieces of evidence so that their relevance can be easily understood is often known as **annotation**.

Keep your evidence in a single sequence with a simple running number on each item.

Using the CAR or CAL forms

When you begin collecting the evidence to put into your portfolio, you should look again at the document you should have received when you registered for your S/NVQ – the Cumulative Assessment Record (CAR) or Candidate Assessment Log (CAL). As well as giving the the full text of the standards which form part of your S/NVQ, this document contains a series of loose-leaf summary forms, one for each standard.

Select the loose-leaf form for the standard you are working towards. In the spaces provided, enter the running numbers for the items of evidence, remembering that each piece of evidence has to meet all of the performance criteria for a particular standard. You can discuss with your assessor whether the evidence you have prepared is sufficient or not. If you have gathered together enough, then stop! You do not get a 'better' S/NVQ if you present more evidence, nor does a lot of evidence in one area compensate for weakness in another.

The loose-leaf forms from the CAR or CAL will help you to organize the evidence in relation to elements and performance criteria. You may find it helpful, in addition, to keep a schedule of the items of evidence, to help you locate documents you want to refer to more than once. Your portfolio should make it easy for you or your assessor to find single items of evidence quickly.

Use the loose-leaf forms from the CAR or CAL to present the evidence in relation to the different standards, keeping the evidence itself in a single numbered sequence. Do not collect more evidence than you need.

Finally, remember that your S/NVQ portfolio can be much more than just a submission for a qualification. It can be a permanent record of your continuing development and career achievements. It can be a useful part of your system for planning and managing your career. But most of all, it can be an achievement in itself – a well-organized, well-presented document which represents the best that you can do, and a important project of which you can be proud.

If you have read right the way through the book up to this point, you should have a good grasp of what the S/NVQ system is all about and how it works. The following chapter makes a few suggestions about what to do next.

6 Next steps

I hope that by now you feel that you understand the S/NVQ system. This chapter makes some suggestions about where to go from here – what steps to take in order to get moving towards an S/NVQ.

Make contact with an assessment centre

If you work for a large organization, such as a local authority or a big company, you may well find that your employer has already registered (or intends to register) as an assessment centre. In this case, your training or personnel office will be able to help you. If, on the other hand, you work in a small organization, or one that employs very few librarians or information workers, you may find that you have to go outside to find a suitable centre. You will be able to obtain details of local assessment centres from Edexcel, OCR, SQA or the ILS Lead Body office.

There will be someone from the assessment centre with whom you can discuss your needs, ambitions and objectives – and who will, at this stage, be acting informally as an advisor. If the assessment centre is not part of your own organization, make sure that your employer knows what you are doing. It is very important to seek your employer's support and approval for your S/NVQ plans.

Get to know the standards

Obtain a copy of the standards. The awarding bodies, Edexcel, OCR and SQA, all publish versions of the standards aimed at candidates and assessment centres. As a candidate (or a potential candidate) you will find these versions helpful, because they put the Units of Competence together in their S/NVQ groupings, and include the definitions for the Units derived from other lead bodies. Another version is published by the lead body itself, and is the official and definitive version – but it covers only the ILS Units and groups them together in a different way.

Read the standards closely. Refer back to Chapter 3 to remind yourself what the different sections of the standard and Unit definitions mean. Remember that the definitions in the standards have been written with great care. The words and sentences used mean exactly what they say – no more and no less – and every sentence is there because it is an important part of the definition. Then, look at the way that different Units are grouped into S/NVQs at different levels, and see how the qualifications differ as you move up from Level 2 to Level 4.

Begin to relate the standards to your own experience

Think about your own competence. Think about what you know you can do – and what you could demonstrate you can do. Think about which elements of competence are already part of your job. Some of the elements will be represented by things you do every day, some by tasks or functions you undertake less frequently.

Next, think about what you could easily learn to do, with a bit of extra practice or training, or perhaps with some additional job experience. Think about which elements are closely related to your job. These elements might represent functions undertaken by close colleagues or associates.

Then think about jobs you have done in the past, and the tasks and functions you undertook then. You will probably find that there are aspects of those jobs which do not constitute part of your present job. Think about which standards could be related to your past experience.

Start thinking about evidence. As you reflect on your areas of competence, think about what evidence you can present. Remember that evidence can be anything that shows you have met the performance criteria: letters, memos, photographs – even videos and tape recordings could count.

Identify your training needs – and plan how you are going to meet them

By now you will have got to know the standards fairly well, and you will probably have found that in order to achieve your S/NVQ, you will have to gain competence in some areas with which you are unfamiliar. It may be that there are some elements in a Unit which represent aspects of a job you have never been called upon to do – or it may be that there is a whole Unit that you have never been involved with. Either way, you have identified an area of competence in which you will have to learn something – and acquire some new skills or refine and practise some existing ones.

Gain the support of your employer

All of this means that you may require some extra training – and will almost certainly need the opportunity to undertake and become competent in work that may be unfamiliar to you. In order to be given that opportunity, you will probably have to secure the cooperation and support of your employer. You will find this much easier if you approach the problem systematically. You should:

- **identify** the areas in which you feel that you are not yet competent, and which you wish to master in order to acquire a Unit or a full S/NVQ;
- **prepare** a realistic training proposal, showing how you could gain the necessary experience without disrupting your own work or that of the organization;
- **justify** your proposal, by showing that you will be able to perform your job better, and thus enhance the performance of the organization as a whole, if you receive the training you believe you need and the qualification you believe you deserve;
- **negotiate** with your employer on the basis of your proposal;
- **agree** a training programme – which will form part of your S/NVQ assessment programme.

Your employer has a direct interest in your training. If you, as an employee, are encouraged to be competent in the broad range of functions that are associated with your job, then you will perform better and the organization as a whole will benefit. If, on the other hand, your training is based only on your immediate tasks, you will only be able to work in a narrow and inflexible way – and the organization will suffer. Most employers will respond positively to a request for training that is well-argued and is part of a clear personal and professional development plan.

However, occasionally candidates will find that their employer is unwilling to cooperate. This can be difficult, and there is no easy answer. If you are unfortunate enough to find yourself in this situation, here are some suggestions:

- Try persuasion. Your employer has a stake in your development, because if your performance improves you will give better value for money. Remember that many employers face demands for quality assurance, and for them, having a staff development policy that includes provision for S/NVQs can be very important.
- Explore the possibility of proceeding without your employer's cooperation. An external assessment centre will be sympathetic towards your situation, and your assessor will understand any difficulties in obtaining evidence. Remember that going along this route will involve you in a lot of extra work – but if you show that you are determined to proceed, your employer may come round in the end!
- If all else fails, consider changing your job. If an organization is not prepared to cooperate with employees who want to improve their skills and gain work-related qualifications, you must ask yourself whether it is worth working for.

Remember – your career and your skills belong to you, not to your employer.

Registering with the assessment centre

When you register, there are certain fees to be paid to Edexcel, OCR or SQA, and possibly also to the assessment centre. Your employer may meet the fees. But if you have to pay them yourself, remember that they are tax-deductible. In most cases, the assessment centre can claim the tax on your behalf, which means that you only pay 75% of the full amount.

After you have registered, you should receive your Cumulative Assessment Record or your Candidate Assessment Log, and you can begin collecting and organizing evidence. You will be given access to all of the systems and facilities described in Chapter 3. When you have got to this stage, you will already be well into the S/NVQ process, and you should find that there are plenty of people who can advise you about your progress and the procedures you should be following.

Good luck!

Reference section

A: Useful addresses

Information and Library Services Lead Body
c/o The Library Association
7 Ridgmount Street
LONDON
WC1E 7AE
Tel: 020 7242 2244
Fax: 020 7242 4640
e-mail: ilslb@dial.pipex.com

The Lead Body maintains a World Wide Web page which
includes information about assessment centres:
http://www.ilsnvq.org.uk/ilsnvq/

Edexcel Foundation
Customer Response Centre
Stewart House
32 Russell Square
LONDON
W1B 5DN
Tel: 020 7393 4500
Fax: 020 7393 4501

Oxford Cambridge RSA Examinations (OCR)
Customer Information Bureau
Westwood Way
COVENTRY
CV4 8HS
Tel: 01203 470033
Fax: 01203 468080

Scottish Qualifications Authority (SQA)
Hanover House
24 Douglas Street
GLASGOW
G2 7NQ
Tel: 0141 248 7900
Fax: 0141 242 2244

Qualifications and Curriculum Authority (QCA)
Newcombe House
45 Notting Hill Gate
LONDON
W11 3JB
Tel: 020 7229 1234
Fax: 020 7229 8526

New telephone codes

Telephone codes are changing during the lifetime of this book. The new codes have been given for all those numbers that are affected, as these will be operational from 1 June 1999. However, please note that before 22 April 2000, when dialling locally, you will need to use the existing local number. For example:

(0171) 636 7543 becomes (020) 7636 7543
From 1 June 1999, use (020) 7637 7543 when dialling from outside the old 0171 area but until 22 April 2000 use 636 7543 when dialling from inside the old 0171 area.

B: Glossary – an S/NVQ jargon-buster

Accreditation: approval by the national bodies QCA and SQA of the procedures for NVQs and SVQs. Three things have to be approved: first, the *occupational standards*; second, the qualifications that derive from them; and third, the appointment of *awarding bodies*.

Annotating evidence: when *evidence* is presented for assessment, it is annotated so that the relevant parts can be easily identified and understood.

Assessment: the process in which judgments are made, on the basis of *evidence*, about a candidate's performance.

Assessment centre: the body which organizes a candidate's *assessment*. An assessment centre can be the company, library or local authority in which a candidate works – or a consortium of organizations, or even a separate entity such as a local college.

Assessor: the person who judges a candidate's performance against the agreed *occupational standards*.

Awarding body: a body appointed to organise an programme of NVQs or SVQs and authorised to award qualifications. In ILS, the awarding bodies are the Edexcel Foundation and Oxford Cambridge RSA Examinations (OCR) for England, Wales and Northern Ireland, and the Scottish Qualifications Authority (SQA) for Scotland.

Candidate Assessment Log (CAL): a document available to every candidate registering for an NVQ with the Edexcel Foundation, which contains details of the *Units* required, together with information about *assessment* procedures and *evidence* requirements.

Credit Accumulation and Transfer Scheme (CATS): the system under which credits made by one *awarding body* are recognised by other awarding bodies. An important component of transferability.

Certificate: the document issued by an awarding body to confirm either that *Units of Competence* have been gained, or that an S/NVQ has been awarded.

Certification: the process of issuing a *certificate*.

Competence: the ability to perform specified kinds of work or fill particular work roles to nationally agreed *standards* in a work situation. Competence is essentially work-related.

Context: the different conditions and circumstances in which a candidate must be able to demonstrate *competence*.

Core skills: certain skills which underpin *competence* and are common across a wide range of areas of work. They are concerned with things like information technology, numeracy, working with others and communication skills. Also known as *key skills*.

Core Units: another term for *Mandatory Units* – Units which are a compulsory part of an S/NVQ. Most S/NVQs are made up of some compulsory Units and a number of Optional Units from among which a choice can be made.

Credit accumulation: the system which enables candidates to accumulate *Units* over time as they move towards a full S/NVQ.

Cumulative Assessment Record (CAR): a document sent to every candidate registering for an S/NVQ with OCR, which contains details of the *Units* required, together with information about *assessment* procedures and *evidence* requirements.

Direct evidence: *evidence* which is produced directly as the result of a candidate's work. This can be either *performance evidence* or *supplementary evidence*.

Element: often used for one of the activities which forms part of a *Unit of Competence* – the smallest piece of work-related activity within the S/NVQ system. Now generally referred to as a *standard* within a *Unit*.

Employment sector: an area of employment in which employees share the same *key purpose* and are engaged on the same or closely related activities. Information and Library Services is an Employment Sector.

Evidence: anything which can be presented as proof of *competence*. Evidence can be written or based on observation, or even derived from simulation. See: *direct evidence, indirect evidence, performance evidence* and *supplementary evidence*.

Evidence indicator: the ILS *occupational standards* specify the types of evidence that should be presented for assessment. These are sometimes referred to as *evidence indicators*.

External verifier: the person appointed by the *awarding body* to check the routines and assessment systems of an *assessment centre*, and ensure that quality is maintained.

Functional analysis: the process of analysing the work undertaken in an *employment sector* in order to determine *Units of Competence* and their *standards*.

General National Vocational Qualification (GNVQ): study programmes and qualifications designed for people not in employment to prepare them for working life. GNVQs are concerned with some of the key areas of knowledge and understanding required in employment.

Indirect evidence: *evidence* of a candidate's performance that is provided by other people – for example, in the form of testimonials or witness statements.

Internal verifier: the person appointed by the *assessment centre* to check the procedures and assessments of *assessors*, and to ensure that quality is maintained.

Key function: one of the subdivisions of a *key purpose*, which breaks an *employment sector*'s mission down into aims and objectives.

Key purpose: the statement of the common mission or goal of all those working in a particular area of employment.

Key role: one of the subdivisions of a *key function*, which breaks an aim or objective into broad areas of work in which all the tasks are related.

Key skills: certain skills which underpin *competence* and are common across a wide range of areas of work. They are concerned with things like information technology, numeracy, working with others and communication skills. Also known as *core skills*.

Lead body: the committee which initially develops the *occupational standards* for an *employment sector*, and then reviews and revises them as necessary. A lead body consists of experienced workers from all parts of the sector together with representatives of professional bodies, trades unions and other interested parties. Lead bodies are sometimes known as *standard-setting bodies*.

Learning and assessment contract: a formal, signed agreement between the candidate and the candidate's employer which sets out the learning and development activities that are needed, and the *assessments* that may be undertaken, for progress towards an S/NVQ.

Learning diary: a document showing how a candidate has progressed, in terms of learning and development, which on a S/NVQ programme.

Level: S/NVQs exist in five levels, with five being the highest. ILS S/NVQs have been accredited for levels two to four only; a level five S/NVQ may be developed in the future, but there is unlikely to be a level one.

Mandatory Units: *Units* which are a compulsory part of a S/NVQ. Most S/NVQs are made up of some compulsory Units and a number of optional units from among which a choice can be made. Sometimes called *Core Units*.

Mentor: a person appointed to help candidates through their development plans and in preparing their *evidence* for *assessment*.

National Council for Vocational Qualifications (NCVQ): now part of the *Qualifications and Curriculum Authority (QCA)*.

National Qualifications Framework: the framework in the UK which relates different types of qualifications together, allowing candidates to progress through GNVQs, vocational schemes or academic schemes.

National Record of Achievement (NRA): a standardized

document file in which can be kept records of all qualifications from school onwards, together with accounts of other achievements and experience. The National Record of Vocational Achievement (NROVA) is a similar file.

National Vocational Qualification (NVQ): a qualification accredited by QCA and based on national standards of competence. An NVQ is composed of a number of *Units of Competence*, and a candidate has to demonstrate competence in a set number of those Units.

NVQ criteria: QCA's published criteria which any NVQs have to meet before they can be accredited. SQA publishes similar criteria for SVQs.

Occupational area: an area of work in which all those involved are engaged in broadly similar tasks.

Occupational standards: the national *standards*, agreed by the relevant *lead body*, which indicate the standards of competence expected of candidates seeking NVQs. Often referred to simply as 'The Standards'. The Standards are also statements of best practice.

OCR: see *Oxford Cambridge RSA Examinations*.

Outcome: sometimes used for one of the activities which forms part of a *Unit of Competence*. Now generally referred to as a *standard* within a Unit.

Oxford Cambridge RSA Examinations (OCR): an *awarding body* for ILS NVQs in England, Wales and Northern Ireland. Formed by the merger of the RSA Examinations Board and the Oxford and Cambridge Examinations Board.

Performance criteria: statements which define what specific outcomes are expected of candidates' performance if they are to be assessed as competent. Performance criteria form part of the definition of a *standard*.

Performance evidence: *evidence* generated directly from a candidate's personal activities. This might be examples of work completed, observation of tasks being undertaken, or responses to a simulated situation.

Performance standards: another term for *occupational standards*.

Personal competence: aspects of a candidate's behaviour that have to be present if the *performance criteria* are to be met. These might include courtesy towards customers, for example, or an awareness of health and safety.

Personal report: a report that places *evidence* in a context by explaining actions or outcomes that are expected in a particular working environment. A personal report can be part of a candidate's evidence.

Portfolio of evidence: a collection of *evidence* of different types, brought together with the necessary explanatory and indexing material, and presented for assessment.

Prior achievement: competent performance that has been achieved before the period of assessment – for example, in a previous job. Evidence of prior achievement can be accepted, provided that it is sufficiently strong to show that the candidate is currently competent.

Process evidence: this involves your assessor looking at how you work. It is a form of *performance evidence*.

Product evidence: the direct output of work you have done. It is one form of *performance evidence*.

Progression: passing through the S/NVQ system and the *National Qualifications Framework* from the lower levels to higher levels, or from one occupational area to another.

Qualification: the formal recognition that a standard of competence or knowledge has been achieved.

Qualifications and Curriculum Authority (QCA): the national body, answerable to the government, which accredits NVQs in England, Wales and Northern Ireland. Part of QCA is the body which used to be called the *National Council for Vocational Qualifications (NCVQ)*.

Range statement: a statement indicating the range of circumstances in which competence in a *standard* must be applied. It forms part of the definition of a standard, and is found under the heading 'Performance Evidence'.

Record of education and training: In Scotland, a certificate issued by SQA to indicate the achievement of SVQ Units and other awards recognised by SQA.

Reference identifier: an identification mark, such as a running number, given to each piece, or sample, of *evidence* to help locate it in a *portfolio*.

RSA Examinations Board: now part of *Oxford Cambridge RSA Examinations*.

Scheme book: a document held by every *assessment centre*, which gives details of all the *Units* and *standards* applying to all of the ILS NVQs, together with information about assessment procedures and evidence requirements.

Scottish Qualifications Authority (SQA): the Scottish equivalent of QCA – the national body which accredits SVQs. Unlike QCA, SQA is an *awarding body* as well, and is the awarding body for ILS SVQs. It used to be called the *Scottish Vocational Education Council (SCOTVEC)*.

Scottish Vocational Education Council (SCOTVEC): now renamed the *Scottish Qualifications Authority (SQA)*.

Scottish Vocational Qualification (SVQ): a qualification accredited by SQA and based on *National Standards of Competence*. An SVQ, like an NVQ, is composed of a number of *Units of Competence*, and a candidate has to demonstrate *competence* in a set number of those Units.

Simulation: in circumstances where a candidate's normal work does not include certain kinds of tasks, simulation may be used to demonstrate *competence*. Simulation involves setting up an 'artificial' situation, and collecting evidence about the candidate's responses and actions. Appendix 1 contains more information about the use of simulation.

Skill: the ability to do something well. A skill can be manual or intellectual. Unlike *competence*, skills can be demonstrated outside the context of work and employment.

Skill transfer: the ability to transfer performance from one context to another.

Standard: one of the activities which forms part of a *Unit of Competence* – the smallest piece of work-related activity within the S/NVQ system. Often referred to as an *element*.

Standard-setting body: the committee which initially develops the *occupational standards* for an *employment sector*, and then reviews and revises them as necessary. A standard-setting body consists of experienced workers from all parts of the sector together with representatives of professional bodies, trades unions and other interested parties. Standard-setting bodies are sometimes known as *lead bodies*.

Standards: see *occupational standards*.

Statement of achievement: the official definition of the *National Standard of Competence* required for the award of a GNVQ.

Statement of competence: the official definition of the *National Standard of Competence* required for the award of an NVQ or an SVQ. It includes the title of the S/NVQ, as well as the *Units* required, together with the associated *performance criteria, range statements* and *underpinning knowledge and understanding*.

Supplementary evidence: *evidence*, usually derived from questioning of the candidate by the *assessor*, or from off-the-job testing, which supports *performance evidence*. It is often concerned with general knowledge and understanding, or *underpinning knowledge and understanding*.

Transferability: the concept that *competence*, once acquired and demonstrated, should be able to be applied in different working environments, thus aiding an individual's job transfers and career progression.

Transparency: The S/NVQ system is open and accessible to all. All *performance standards* are published and openly available. *Assessors* have, if asked, to give reasons to candidates for their assessment judgements. This is referred to as transparency.

Underpinning Knowledge and Understanding (UKU): this term is sometimes used for the theoretical knowledge or understanding which is necessary before a candidate can be considered to be competent. A statement of knowledge and understanding forms part of the definition of a *standard*, and is found in the section headed 'You understand . . .'.

Unit of Competence: the smallest grouping of work skills for which it is possible to gain certification under the S/NVQ system. A Unit is composed of a number of standards. An S/NVQ is composed of a number of Units.

Verification: the process of monitoring which ensures that the whole S/NVQ process is being carried out as it should. *Assessors'* judgments about candidates are subject to verification.

Verifier: a person who is responsible for *verification*. Verifiers can be *internal* (appointed by an assessment centre) or *external* (appointed by an awarding body). They monitor the judgements of *assessors* about candidates; *external verifiers* also monitor the procedures of *assessment centres*.

Appendix 1: Assessment guidance
[for a Level 2 S/NVQ in Information and Library Services]

Assessment Guidance

Performance Evidence

An NVQ/SVQ is awarded when a person has achieved all the Units of Competence in the award. For example in this qualification, the candidate has to achieve a total of six Units. Candidates achieve Units when they bring forward evidence that meets the standards (sometimes called "Elements" or "Outcomes") in the Unit. For example in Unit IL2/1 *Maintain the arrangement of material* there are two standards:

IL2/1.1 Sort and re-place material

IL2/1.2 Check the condition and arrangement of material

The evidence the candidate brings forward must be evidence of performance – what she or he can do, not just what he or she knows. The evidence required for each standard is described alongside the standard itself. For example:

You show that you can . . .

IL2/1.1 Sort and re-place material

Performance Evidence

To achieve the standard, you produce evidence from your work that you can sort and re-place material on two occasions.

As you can see, this states clearly what the candidate has to do to be judged competent in 'sorting and replacing material'. It is called performance evidence simply because it shows what the individual is capable of achieving in a real work role.

In the example above, the specification goes on to describe the kind of evidence required:

> **You show in your performance that:**
> R1 you can sequence material either by classification or by subject grouping
> R2 you can re-place at least one of the following types of material:
> - printed material, such as books and journals
> - recorded material, such as audio tapes, videos or CDs
> - filmed material, such as microfiches or filmed images
> R3 . . . in the following types of storage:
> - open storage, such as shelves or racks
> - closed storage, such as drawers, cupboards or cabinets

What the assessor does with the evidence
The assessor judges and decides: that is, she/he

- **judges** each sample against the standard;
- reviews all the evidence to **decide** whether the candidate meets the standard.

Each sample must be judged against **all** the criteria in a standard. Each criterion is simply an aspect of performance which is critical to performing competently. Taken together, the criteria describe the difference between a competent performance and one that is not. So in IL2/1.1, the assessor will judge the way the candidate sorts and re-places material. In this case, the assessor will have to see the candidate's work. This includes observing the candidate. The assessor must decide (with the candidate) whether it will be necessary to observe performance on every occasion. What is essential is that the evidence for each sample **must** meet **all** the criteria in the standard. In the example, these are:

So, you show that you . . .

1   sort and re-place material accurately and with minimum disruption to users
2   re-place material tidily and in its correct place
3   handle and position material safely
4   note and correct promptly any errors in sequencing the material
5   get appropriate assistance to resolve difficulties you have in re-placing material

---

The assessor looks at the evidence which the candidate produces, and decides whether it meets **all** these criteria.

When observing a candidate at work, the assessor looks at what the candidate does and checks that the performance meets the criteria.

When the assessor is looking at evidence in written form (such as a report or a log of activity kept by the candidate), exactly the same criteria are used to judge it. This means that good communication and planning is needed between the assessor and the candidate, to ensure that written evidence is presented in a way which enables the assessor to test it against the criteria without having to ask for more information.

When **judging each sample**, the assessor is deciding whether the evidence is:

• authentic – i.e. actually produced by the candidate;

- meets all the criteria;
- relates to one or more of the contexts defined in the range statements;
- confirms that the candidate has the required underpinning knowledge (see Knowledge Evidence below).

When the assessor **makes an assessment decision** about the candidate's competence, s/he examines all the evidence available (that is, all the samples) to determine:

- whether the evidence, as a whole, covers all the **range statements** in each standard;
- whether the samples indicate **consistency** in competent performance;
- whether there are **enough samples** of evidence on which to base an inference of competence.

The **range statements** describe different working conditions in which the candidate is expected to maintain standards of performance. You can tell what these are because they are described in the performance evidence as R1, R2, etc. These say whether the candidate must produce performance evidence for each item listed, or for a selection.

In the example above, each candidate has to show that:

R2 you can re-place at least one of the following types of material:
- printed material, such as books and journals
- recorded material, such as audio tapes, videos or CDs
- filmed material, such as microfiches or filmed images

This means that the candidate has to produce one sample of performance evidence.

However, the candidate must also show that she/he can deal with all types of material. This can be done by showing that she/he knows how to deal with them – that is, that they have the underpinning knowledge needed.

So, when planning evidence collection, the assessor and candidate should agree which material the candidate deals with most frequently at work and select the two which will appear in the performance evidence. The assessor can then decide how to check that the candidate understands how to identify the other types – usually by questioning the candidate.

If in doubt about this, the assessor should ask their internal verifier or seek the advice of the Awarding Body.

Consistency means that the individual is likely to achieve the standard in their work role in the different contexts defined by the range and over time. The assessor must judge how long a time period is enough to be confident that the candidate can perform reliably to the standard. The statement of what evidence is required refers to this:

> To achieve the standard, you produce evidence from your work that you can sort and re-place material on two occasions.

The assessor must, therefore, decide what will be a reasonable period of time. To decide this, the assessor must know about the candidate's job, and the circumstances in which the candidate works. Four principles should guide the assessor's judgement of what constitutes a reasonable period of time:

- The time period should be long enough for the candidate to produce the samples of evidence required, across the range (see 1 above);

- The time period should be linked to the complexity of the candidate's work. If it is highly repetitive and simple (such as filing), it is likely that a short time period will be enough. If it is more complex and non-routine, it may time some time before the assessor can safely infer that the candidate can perform consistently;
- The time period should not so long that the candidate is discouraged from collecting the evidence, or demotivated because of what she/he may see as unnecessary delay before being judged competent;
- All candidates must be treated equally and impartially. It may be necessary for some candidates to take longer to produce the required evidence than others (for example, because of working conditions or the specific nature of the candidate's job), but these differences should be kept to a minimum, and it must be clear to the candidate that the reasons are related to consistency of performance. Assessors are expected to use their own experience of the work the candidate does to decide this. They are also expected to be disciplined in avoiding unfair treatment of candidates, or in letting their own pre-conceptions lead them to demand either too much or too little evidence.

The assessor decides that **enough evidence** has been collected when he/she can make a **safe inference** of competence. 'Safe' does not mean 'over-cautious'. It simply means that it is a judgement which other assessors, the internal verifier and the external verifier are likely to agree with, or which can be successfully defended (by reference to the evidence) if challenged. Once again, assessors are expected to avoid personal bias in judging whether evidence is sufficient. They are also expected to be consistent when making these judgements for different candidates.

Collecting the Evidence

When planning assessments, both the assessor and the candidate should use the Performance Evidence shown in this publication to identify opportunities to collect evidence which arises naturally in the candidate's job. The best of these can be used to observe the candidate achieving the standard.

If it not possible to collect all the required samples by observation, the assessor must consider how else the candidate should produce the evidence. There are a number of different ways of doing this; for example:

- the candidate may keep a diary or log describing work related to the standard;
- evidence can be used from those who have observed the candidate achieving the standard – this is known as witness testimony;
- the candidate may be able to bring forward relevant evidence from recent past experience.

Sometimes *product evidence* is required – that is evidence in the form of things the candidate has produced in the course of their work. For example in IL2/1.1, the evidence may take the form of the records produced by the candidate.

Matching the Evidence to the Criteria

It is not appropriate to collect evidence against individual criteria. Nor is it efficient, because it can lead to producing more evidence than is needed, which can demoralise candidates and over-burden assessors.

It will happen, occasionally, that, when the assessor observes the candidate, the performance will not produce evidence which matches all the criteria. As far as possible, these circumstances should be avoided by good assessment planning.

For example, in IL2/11.1 (Plan to set up displays to specification), criterion 1 is:

> identify the purpose and requirements of the display from the available information

This may have happened before the assessor observes the candidate. Good planning will spot instances like this, and the candidate should be asked to have evidence ready that they have met this requirement.

Sometimes a criterion describes a situation which does not always arise. In IL2/1.1, ('Sort and re-place material') criteria 4 and 5 are:

> (you) note and promptly correct any errors in sequencing the material
> (you) get appropriate assistance to resolve difficulties you have in re-placing material

Neither may occur when the candidate is observed by the assessor. When this happens, the assessor will still need evidence that the candidate's performance meets the requirement. This evidence can be produced in different ways; for example:

- by asking the candidate what they would do, if the circumstance arose (What if . . . questions);
- by collecting witness testimony;
- by using evidence from the candidate's recent past experience.

Sometimes, the circumstances of a candidate's job are such that not all the samples of evidence can be collected in the normal working environment. For examples, the pattern of a candidate's work may be such that it will take too long to collect the evidence from the job itself: or it may be that the candidate does not have opportunities to meet the standard in their normal job.

Other ways in which evidence can be collected in these circumstances include:

- through arranging a secondment;
- through specially arranged project work;
- through bringing forward evidence from past experience;
- through a simulation – but see the section on simulation below.

These should be used in exceptional circumstances, and assessors should discuss the use with the internal verifier.

Types of performance evidence

Performance evidence can be:

- naturally occurring – that is, evidence produced in the normal course of doing the job;
- simulated – that is, from contexts specially designed to enable the candidate's performance to be assessed.
- previous achievements – that is, the candidate may be able to bring forward evidence from previous work experience to show that they are still competent to the standard – see *Prior Achievement* below.

Using simulations

Normally performance evidence should be collected from everyday work performance. Evidence of this sort is usually of better quality and more reliable. It is also more cost-effective to collect evidence that arises naturally from work in this way. However, it is not always possible or feasible to do this. It is likely that some simulation may be needed, when:

- it may take too long to wait for the evidence to arise: e.g. it may be an aspect of performance which occurs infrequently. An example of this may be evidence of how to

deal with emergencies
* the context may not permit the evidence to be collected,
  or the performance to be observed – e.g. it may be
  impractical or counter-productive to observe someone
  seeking feedback on their work performance.

Be warned, however! The term 'simulation' is used in different ways by different people. Six different methods are shown on the next page. When people use the term 'simulation', they may mean any of these.

Table 1 *Types of Simulation*

1 Rehearsals	A complex simulation of a complete working environment. Often used in the learning process, but may also be used for assessment. In rehearsals, almost all aspects of the real environment are present – equipment, products, locations, people, etc. Often used to observe performance, but there may be product outcomes as well.
2 Role plays	A representation of an interaction in which one or more people "act" out parts in order to stimulate a response from the person being assessed. The "actor" usually works from a script. Sometimes (usually) the assessee knows that the other(s) are playing a role. Sometimes (as with mystery shoppers) they may not know. Outcomes and processes may be observed or recorded.
3 Work Project	A complex activity usually involving a number of associated outcomes and processes. Projects normally include data collection, investigation, analysis, calculation, interpretation, synthesis, presentation of findings and formatting of written reports. They may also be referred to as assignments.
4 Off-Job Project	The same as 3, except that the project is done away from the working environment, and may be based on hypothetical data and information.
5 Job Placement	Temporary placement in another work role with the same employer, and which is not part of the individual's normal job. Can be used to assess any aspect of competence.
6 Work Placement	Temporary placement in a work environment in which the candidate is not an employee.

(Source: Bob Mansfield & Nanci Downey: The Simulation of Evidence in National Vocational Qualifications – Draft Guidance. Prime R&D for NCVQ 1995)

Generally, you should ask yourself the following questions before considering producing evidence from simulations:

- does the individual's workplace offer no opportunities to collect the evidence you need for a whole unit or standard?
- are there limited opportunities to collect evidence against all the aspects defined in the performance evidence?
- is it unethical, too dangerous or too time-consuming to collect evidence in the workplace?

If the answers are 'Yes', then you should consider using simulations, starting with looking at the possibilities of job rotation or work placement.

Prior Achievement
Evidence of prior achievement can be used when it can be shown to support a judgement that the candidate can still achieve the standards. So, the assessor must be satisfied that evidence of prior achievement is sufficiently reliable to justify saying that the candidate is **currently** competent. Please see the Employment NTO Unit D36 (*Advise and Support Candidates to Identify Prior Achievement*) for the standards which apply to helping candidates to produce such evidence.

Types of evidence
Performance evidence can be what the individual actually produces, or the way the individual achieves the standard. One is called **product evidence** and the other **process evidence**.

   Product evidence is tangible – you can look at it, feel it, taste it (in the case of food!). Product evidence might be an assembled display, a report or a written risk assessment. Products can be inspected and the candidate can be asked questions about them.

Process evidence describes the way the candidate has achieved an outcome – how they went about it. This may be, for example, the way the candidate deals with users, or the way she/he works with others. This usually means observing the candidate in action. On balance most of the evidence needed in Information and Library Services is process evidence.

Evidence collection methods

Performance evidence may be collected in different ways – by observation of the candidate's performance, by examining what the candidate produces (such as documents) and, with simulations, by skill tests, competence tests, projects and assignments. When used to collect performance evidence, observations of performance might come directly from being there, or by recording the performance, for example on video or audiotape. However evidence is collected, please remember more than one method should be used, in order to assure the quality of the evidence and to make reliable assessment decisions.

It makes sense to plan evidence collection so that what the candidate does, in the normal course of their job, can be related to different standards and units. Care, however, must be taken not to over-use evidence – i.e. to 'stretch' a piece of evidence so that it is made to 'fit' a variety of standards. If this happens, the assessment decisions are likely to be challenged by the verifiers – and, of course, the competence of the individual will be in doubt.

The really important judgement the assessor and candidate must make is to decide what standard or standards actually apply to the daily activities of the job. These should be things to concentrate on when planning evidence collection and assessment and when monitoring the candidate's progress.

So look for opportunities in the candidate's job when evidence can be collected against several standards at the same time – but don't do this at the expense of good evidence – that is, evidence which clearly relates to a standard and which is reliable and valid.

One way of planning which methods to use is to use the following procedure:

- Go through the Performance Evidence requirements with the candidate, and ask the candidate to identify when, in their work, they do what the performance evidence requires.
- Draw up (or get the candidate to draw up) a list of the opportunities for generating evidence at work identified in this way. This may well show that, at certain times, or when performing certain tasks, the candidate can generate evidence which applies to most or all the standards in a unit of competence, or, indeed, to several standards in different units. This will make evidence collection efficient, and make the best use of the assessor's time.
- Use the list to decide when the best assessment opportunities arise, and use these to agree the assessment schedule with the candidate.

The list you produce could look something like this:

Opportunity	Evidence Generated	Relevant to:								
		1.1	1.2	1.3	2.1	2.2	3.1	3.2	3.3	Etc
1										
2										
3										
4										

Knowledge evidence

Being able to achieve a standard means putting the knowledge you have to work. Along with each standard, there is a description of the knowledge each person should use if they are to perform competently. This is shown in the **Knowledge Evidence** section.

It should not be necessary to test all the candidate's knowledge separately. The performance evidence should show that the candidate knows what she or he is doing. When this is not the case, or if the assessor is not convinced from the performance evidence, it may be necessary to check the individual's knowledge separately.

The Awarding Bodies should give guidance on how best to handle this. The important principle is that the candidate's competence must be judged against the available performance evidence. Knowledge evidence is useful when deciding the quality of performance evidence, but must not be used in isolation to judge competence or as an alternative to performance evidence.

Equality of opportunity

Equality of access to fair and valid assessment is a guarantee for all candidates for NVQs/SVQs/Units. This may mean making arrangements for candidates with special assessment needs – for example, for those working at a distance from the assessment centre. Candidates' work patterns should not become a barrier to assessment, the organisation of which may have to be flexible. In the same way, special arrangements may be necessary for candidates with a disability. For example, a candidate who is unable, through disability, to produce oral or written evidence, must be allowed to use the method they normally use as a substitute for the required form of communication.

Steps in the assessment process
Assessment is the last step in a process. It is important to be clear what all the steps are:

1 PLAN EVIDENCE COLLECTION AND ASSESS-MENT
2 COLLECT EVIDENCE OF COMPETENT PER-FORMANCE
3 JUDGE EVIDENCE
4 GIVE FEEDBACK TO THE CANDIDATE
5 DETERMINE WHETHER SUFFICIENT EVI-DENCE HAS BEEN PRESENTED
  [repeat 3 and 4 until sufficient evidence is available. Then. . .]
6 MAKE AN ASSESSMENT DECISION AND GIVE FEEDBACK TO THE CANDIDATE.

Appendix 2: How the ILS S/NVQ standards were developed

You will have seen from Chapter 3 that the S/NVQ system is based on Units which form clearly identifiable segments of work. The division into Units is not arbitrary. In the first place, a Unit is intended to be the smallest segment of work which it is possible to define without losing coherence. And in the second place, Units are related to each other within a hierarchy which is designed so that all aspects of the work of a particular sector are covered. When S/NVQs are being devised for a sector, a study is undertaken to determine exactly what it is that people working in the sector do, and to prepare both the hierarchy and the list of Units. In the case of the ILS sector, this was one of the first tasks of the lead body.

A firm of specialist consultants was appointed to manage the study. They ran many workshops all over the country, involving people working at all levels of seniority in a very wide range of types of library and information unit. As well as public and academic libraries, the workshops covered all kinds of commercial libraries as well as archives, tourist information centres and indexers. At the workshops, those attending were asked to talk about their work and to agree common principles and activities, and from the results of their discussion a first draft of the Unit hierarchy was developed. This technique of investigating working practice is known as **functional analysis**, and the resulting hierarchy is known as a **functional map**.

The functional map went through a number of drafts, with each draft being discussed and modified both by members of the lead body and in further workshops. At the same time, the information about working practices was being used to draw up elements, performance criteria, range statements and all the other parts of the Unit definitions. The end result was a final functional map, which formed the basis of the first set of ILS standards published by the lead body in 1985. During this process, the RSA Examinations Board and SCOTVEC were appointed by the lead body as the Awarding Body to launch the ILS S/NVQs.

The S/NVQ system requires that occupational standards are regularly revised and updated. Accordingly, the first functional map was revised and used as the basis for an updated set of standards, published in 1999. During this process, the lead body appointed the Edexcel Foundation as a third awarding body; and allowed for the change in name of the remaining awarding bodies – RSA's to OCR and SCOTVEC's to SQA. Having published the revised standards and approved the changes in the qualifications, the main committee of the lead body is now dormant, and will not meet until it is time to revise the standards again in 2002. However, the Lead Body office and administrative functions are being maintained by the Library Association.

In a functional map, Units are organised according to their relationship with each other. All Units are about competence, but not all competences are exercised at the same level, and Units next to each other on the functional map might be of very different levels. Consequently, Units have to be reorganized into S/NVQs. Three ILS S/NVQs were initially devised – respectively at Levels 2, 3 and 4 – and were then piloted, with real candidates and assessors. After the pilot, some details were revised, and then the three S/NVQs, together with separate ones (with the addition of extra Units) for Tourist Information Centres and Archives, were presented to NCVQ and SCOTVEC for accreditation. After the 1998 revision of the occupational standards, a new set of S/NVQs, with OCR, Edexcel and SQA as awarding bodies, were accredited.

The key document in the development and revision of ILS S/NVQs, therefore, is the functional map. There is no space here to show the map in its entirety, nor to discuss it in detail. However, the nature of the hierarchy of standards and Units can be illustrated by following through from the top of the hierarchy 'tree' down to the point where we encounter the element we discussed in detail in Chapter 3.

All sectors of employment that have developed a set of occupational standards for S/NVQs have agreed a **key purpose**, which defines the scope of the sector and the overall mission of its members, and which is the highest point of the hierarchy. The key purpose of Information and Library Services is:

> To anticipate, determine, stimulate and satisfy
> the needs of existing and potential users for
> access to information in an ethical manner.

Everything in the ILS standards refers back to this key purpose and is derived from it. Associated with the key purpose there is a pattern of functions, roles and job units that spreads out, like the branches of a tree, until it reaches individual tasks and activities.

This key purpose is used to assist in the development and revision of ILS S/NVQs, as a way of ensuring that the qualifications do not lose sight of the overall objective of all those who work in information and library services.

After the key purpose there are two **key functions**. They are to:

- assist users of information/material
- make information/material available for users.

You will immediately see that these functions refer respectively to activities centred on users and those centred on materials or information and information sources. Each key function is again subdivided into a further two **key roles**, which break the user- and materials-centred functions down further into broad areas of activity. The first key function divides into:

- supply information/material to user
- support users in obtaining information/material.

The second divides into:

- develop and improve range of information/material
- maintain information/material for use.

Then each of these four key roles is again subdivided into Units of Competence. The Unit we looked at in Chapter 3 was called *Provide information/material* to user. It forms part of the first key role (*supply information/material to user*) of the first key function. In its turn, as we have seen, the Unit is divided into elements, one of which (*obtain information/material from external provider*), is the element we have examined in close detail.

Index